THE MODERN AFRICAN ELITE OF SOUTH AFRICA

The Modern African Elite of South Africa

Lynette Dreyer

St. Martin's Press   New York

First published in the United States of America in 1989

Printed in Hong Kong

ISBN 0–312–01675–1

Library of Congress Cataloging-in-Publication Data
Dreyer, Lynette, 1949–
The modern African elite of South Africa / Lynette Dreyer.
    p. cm.
Based on author's thesis (Ph. D.)—University of Stellenbosch,
1987.
Bibliography: p.
Includes index.
ISBN 0–312–01675–1 : $35.00
1. Elite (Social sciences)—South Africa. 2. South Africa—Social
conditions—1961–   I. Title.
HN801.Z9E436 1989   88–7048
305.5'2'0968—dc19   CIP

Contents

List of Tables

Acknowledgements

I am indebted to a number of people for assistance at various stages of this project – those whom I approached for advice as well as the sixty people who agreed to be interviewed. All gave freely of their time. The sixty opinion-leaders graciously opened up and let me into their lives of ordinariness and greatness and would no doubt balk at being referred to as 'elite'.

The following organizations kindly granted permission for the reproduction of extracts from their publications: Southern Book Publishers for Table 2.1; Bureau of Market Research at the University of South Africa for Table 3.10; Markinor for Tables 4.15 and 4.17; and the Human Sciences Research Council for Table 3.12 and material from its report *The South African Society: Realities and Future Prospects*.

This book is based on a thesis submitted in 1987 for a doctoral degree at the University of Stellenbosch entitled *The Urbanized African Social Elites of South Africa* under the supervision of S. P. Cilliers, Professor of Sociology.

LYNETTE DREYER

Glossary

Bantustans: see *Homelands*.

Bush universities: Colloquial name for universities established in the homelands to train Africans within the context of their ethnic group.

The *conjugal family* system refers to the Western-type of nuclear family consisting of husband and wife and their dependant children living as one household.

Consanguinity refers to a social relationship based on descent from a common ancestor.

Differentiation refers to a process of societal development whereby social structures divide functionally and separate societal institutions evolve. For example, traditional households which are simultaneously residential, socializing and production units shed some of their socializing and production functions while, *inter alia*, educational and industrial systems develop.

An *extended family* consists of two or more nuclear families related consanguineously often including different generations and single relatives.

The *family of orientation* is the family an individual grows up in, while the *family of procreation* is the one the individual forms by marrying and having children.

Homelands are traditional tribal areas within South Africa's borders which have been turned into political entities and having varying degrees of sovereignty. They are also known as Bantustans or national states. Some of them have reached such a level of political autonomy that they are regarded by the South African government as independent states.

Inkatha is a national cultural organization established by traditional Zulu leaders.

Lobola is a traditional custom among the Africans of Southern Africa whereby goods pass from the husband's to the wife's family as part of the marriage contract.

National states: see *Homelands*.

Pass is the colloquial name for the identity or reference book that every African was legally required to have on his person at all times. It contained details of, *inter alia*, his ethnic extraction and residential rights which determined the legality of his presence at any particular place at any particular time. It was abandoned with the rest of the influx control system during 1986.

Robben Island refers to a maximum security prison previously used for the incarceration of political offenders.

Societal community is a sociological term referring more or less to the core identity of a society.

Volk is an Afrikaans word literally meaning 'people'. When used in this form in English it refers to the Afrikaner people as a distinct cultural group.

1 Introduction

PREAMBLE

This book presents a profile of the top echelon of the African community in South Africa – a sector of society known in international sociological literature as the 'elite'. It concentrates specifically on the modern social elite which are also sometimes referred to as 'opinion-leaders'.

In keeping with the practice in the literature, the concept 'elite' is used to describe a category of people irrespective of the institutional sector to which they belong. At the same time, members of the elite representing different sectors are described with an adjective: for example, the business elite or religious elite. In other words, the business and religious elites are components of the collective social elite. This usage is similar to the usage of the concept 'people', which may be used as in 'the people of South Africa', 'the peoples of South Africa' as well as the 'Black, White, etc. people of South Africa'.

Although the Africans refer to themselves as 'Blacks', the appelation 'Africans' was preferred in this book to distinguish them from the other population groups that are often included in the term 'Black'.

'South Africa' is taken to be the geographical area of the country as in 1960, in other words including Transkei, Bophuthatswana, Venda and Ciskei, as it is regarded as one societal system. When the 'Republic of South Africa' (RSA) is referred to, these four areas are excluded.

THE AFRICANS IN SOUTH AFRICAN SOCIETY

To grasp the role of the African elite within the African community and broader South African society, it is necessary first of all to place the African community itself within South African society. As the position of the African community is largely the result of historical forces, this presentation is handled historically.[1]

The legacy of the history of South Africa is a heterogenous population comprising Africans (20.9 million in 1980), Whites (4.5 million), so-called Coloureds (2.6 million) and Indians (0.8 million).

1

The earliest surviving inhabitants of South Africa were the San (Bushmen) who lived a nomadic life as hunters and gatherers. They were later joined by the Khoikhoi (Hottentots) and African groups speaking Bantu languages who settled in various parts of South Africa and followed their own traditional lifestyles before the arrival of the Whites.

The interaction between these groups was at times characterized by conflict. The Bushmen, in particular, were ousted by the incoming African chiefdoms. Interaction between these groups was mainly determined by economic factors, especially the acquisition and safe-guarding of hunting grounds and pastures, livestock and agricultural land. There was also increasing commercial contact and social inte-gration, especially between the San and Khoikhoi and between the Khoikhoi and the Africans.

The San, Khoikhoi and African tribes were not homogeneous groups. Each was in turn divided into separate communities with their own specific interests, leaders and circumstances. There was a dynamic interaction between these communities based essentially on good neighbourliness but which also included episodes of conflict.

The settlement of Whites in South Africa had an important influ-ence on this dynamism. Not only did it signify the addition of a further group to the existing ones, but the Whites also brought their European values and customs with them. This included foreign capital and irrevocably linked relations between the various groups to foreign interests.

From 1652, White colonial rule was established at the Cape and was gradually extended to the interior until the whole of South Africa was under colonial control. For nearly two and a half centuries South Africa (with the exception of the two Boer republics for about fifty years) was under colonial rule. For economic and military reasons, the Dutch East India Company and later the British government established and maintained authority over South Africa. Colonial control was extended to include all indigenous inhabitants so that all the groups in the region were in due course subjected to the govern-ment at the Cape.

Simultaneously with the establishment of European colonial rule, a White colonist population emerged in South Africa with permanent interests under the control of and sometimes in conflict with the colonial power. The White colonists gradually developed a strong political consciousness and demanded greater participation in the government of the country as well as in the control of the national economy. In due course a specific group, the Afrikaners, developed from the colonist population and they, in time, developed a unique national consciousness. It was the Afrikaners – especially the Afrikaner border farmers – who opposed the colonial authorities and for various reasons moved away from British rule in the Cape colony to establish independent states in the interior. Afrikaner nationalism came strongly to the fore in the second half of the nineteenth century in the face of British imperialism. This led to two wars (the First War of Independence and the Anglo-Boer War) between the Afrikaners and the British.

After the British occupation of the Cape in 1806, a significant number of English-speaking colonists settled in South Africa to become permanent residents of the country. Although British-orientated, they soon acquired a South African identity. They did not identify with the Afrikaners, but social and economic contact between the groups was common. Significant numbers of French and German immigrants also arrived in South Africa at an early stage of White settlement, followed eventually by groups from numerous other European countries.

A characteristic of South African society during this period was its typical frontier nature. The Whites, in the process of expansion into the interior, came into contact with the Khoikhoi, San and Africans. This contact was typified by competition for land and water and a struggle for supremacy. In the early phases of contact none of the groups succeeded in dominating the others. Political and social relations were fluid and all parties enjoyed equal status. As the Whites established their authority over the indigenous communities, the latter lost their land and became subject to White control. Labour played an increasingly important role and the status of the Africans changed from free to subordinate labourers.

The establishment of White authority over Africans was a process in which the colonial authorities and White colonists united against the indigenous population. Only late in the nineteenth century was White authority indusputably established over the Africans.

African reaction to White expansion was divergent. Some groups co-operated with the Whites, for example the Barolong. Others, for example the Xhosa and Zulu, violently resisted, with the result that there was constant conflict between the Whites and the Africans in the border areas. African resistance to White domination was for a long time unco-ordinated and each group tried to oppose the Whites on its own. The first efforts towards co-ordinated resistance only materialized late in the nineteenth century.

The Africans who came into contact with Whites incorporated aspects of the White lifestyle into their own in varying degrees. Another important influence came from the missionaries, who disseminated Christian Western values and brought education to remote rural areas. Consequently from an early stage in South African history there were Africans all along the traditional–modern continuum, with the modernized group growing as time went by with more and more entering professions and skilled occupations.

One of the major factors that was to determine the relationships between the various groups was the gradual growth of an assumption of White superiority and African subordination. There was a large degree of equality between Whites and other groups in early Cape society. Later, however, a legal, and especially a social, distinction was drawn between the groups, so that differentiation on the basis of race and colour became characteristic of South African society. Various factors were responsible for this: among others, cultural, religious and class differences as well as slavery and conflict. This distinction was eventually embodied in legislation.

Generally speaking, the British authorities and colonists were more liberal in their attitude towards other groups than those in the Boer republics. The non-White groups did not have citizenship status in these republics and were not accepted as equals. Yet, although there was a considerable degree of political, social and economic differentiation between the Whites and other groups which led to segregation measures and attitudes, total segregation, particularly in the economic field, was never possible.

Owing to the social equality in early Cape society and the fluid conditions of the border situation in the interior, legal marriages and numerous instances of cohabitation and miscegenation between members of the different population groups occurred. This association between Whites, slaves, Africans, San and Khoikhoi resulted in the development of a group, who were later commonly known as Coloureds and who followed a lifestyle closer to that of the Whites than that of any of the other groups. While some of these people initially acquired equal status with the Whites, the majority, however, had no status and worked for Whites as labourers. The Coloureds have never been a homogeneous group.

In the early phases of the colonial period, before the Whites occupied the interior of South Africa, there was dynamic interaction between the different African population groups. Political development and an increase in numbers intensified the competition for land. This led to friction and conflict that sometimes resulted in drastic political and social changes. The crystallizing of a few big and powerful tribes and a variety of smaller ones was a feature of the period. The political, social and commercial relations between these communities were eventually strongly influenced by the coming of the Whites.

The first Indians came to South Africa in 1860 as contract labourers for the sugar plantations in Natal, and were later followed by Indian traders. The immigration of Indians was stopped early in the twentieth century. Most Indians reside in Natal and virtually all are descendants of the original settlers. Although they have adopted some aspects of the dominant White lifestyle, their own lifestyle has remained predominantly Indian, though modernized.

The discovery of diamonds and gold and the concomitant industrial growth brought about vast changes in South African society. Africans streamed to the industrial centres in large numbers, in turn increasing the number exposed to modernizing influences. On the one hand, this caused social problems in the reserves owing to the absence of economically active males, while, on the other, it led to poor social conditions in the African residential areas of the industrial centres.

A factor that had a very real influence on South African history was the strong upsurge of Afrikaner nationalism and the establishment of the political authority of the Afrikaner in 1948. This gave rise to the passing of a variety of laws in terms of which the ideology of apartheid (later called separate development) was defined and enforced, thereby formalizing previously informal segregation. The objective was total segregation between Whites and others and the insurance that the White group remained dominant in the modern sector. A central part of the policy was the expansion of the African reserves where traditional lifestyles predominated, and where Africans were to express political and social rights and eventually gain independence from South Africa. This was realised in the Transkei, Bophuthatswana, Venda and Ciskei. Laws were enacted to prevent Africans settling outside the reserves and to persuade others to move to the reserves. Great emphasis was placed on the differences between the Africans and the Whites, the traditional origins of the Africans and the differences between the African groups.

For many years after the establishment of Nationalist rule only the statutorily determined White population group was directly represented in Parliament. Before 1983 legislative authority was vested solely in the White parliament. This White parliament proposed political and constitutional autonomy for the reserves which had been established for the various African groups on an ethnic basis. The White parliament also created government institutions for the Coloureds and Indians, i.e. the Coloured Representative Council and the South African Indian Council, both of which were later abandoned.

The separation of the racial groups was further supported by various laws, including, among others, the Group Areas Act (36 of 1966), the Bantu Education Act (47 of 1953), the Reservation of Separate Amenities Act (49 of 1953) and the since repealed Prohibition of Political Interference Act (51 of 1968), to ensure that the different population groups resided and conducted their lifestyle and politics separately. The intention of all this was that each population group would evolve into a separate community with a separate organizational structure. In practice, however, greatest emphasis was placed on the separation of the Whites from all of the non-Whites collectively. This had the result that while Africans were originally supposed to become accommodated in geographically segregated societies, to be eventually politically organized as independent national states, an increasing proportion of the African population became permanently urbanized and economically integrated into the modern industrial economy, while being socially segregated and totally excluded from participation in the formal power structures of the White-dominated modern urban society.

Rising domestic conflict and pressure from abroad led to the most important constitutional change since the unification of South Africa in 1910, namely the adoption of a new constitution, Act 110 of 1983. Where the South African constitutional dispensation had previously followed an adaptation of the Westminster form, the new constitution introduced an executive head of state, separate legislative chambers for Whites, Coloureds and Indians, and bound parliament, both institutionally and functionally, to the procedure of agreement of all three parliamentary chambers. However, it left the constitutional position of the African community unchanged.

This led to increased and continuing conflict within South African society. The conflict mainly concerned political and economic power and social equality. Its nature was also different from that of the previous phases, namely a shift from an unco-ordinated to a more co-ordinated resistance built around organizations such as the African National Congress, the Pan African Congress, the Azanian People's Organization and the United Democratic Front.

The present situation is very volatile, as increasing conflict on the one hand and a re-evaluation of the policy of separate development on the other, have forced the Whites to reassess the political dispensation. A new element of conflict has emerged in that a section of the White community has been mobilized against the inclusion of Africans in the central decision-making structures of South African society.

According to government statements, the future political and constitutional position of the African population enjoys high priority. The most important development to date has been the acceptance by the government that the Africans are citizens of a common South Africa and entitled to participation in all spheres of society.

To summarize: Over at least the last three generations the Africans have become incorporated into the White-dominated modern societal system on a racially differentiated basis. Although excluded from the formal power system, a social hierarchy has developed within the modern African community alongside the hierarchies in the traditional sector on the one hand and the White sector on the other. Status differentiation within the African hierarchy based on rating by others has resulted in a category of people known in the sociological literature as a social elite being formed at the top of the hierarchy. In some limited cases, for example parts of the religious sector, Africans have reached the top of racially integrated organizations, and besides being part of the African social elite, can also be regarded as members of the broader South African social elite. This book is concerned with this African social elite in the modern African sector of the White-dominated South African society.

TOWARDS DEFINING THE ELITE

Since the early writings in sociology, scholars have studied the phenomenon of elites. The first theoretician was Mosca, who in 1896 described man's primary motivation as a struggle for pre-eminence rather than a struggle for survival. He was followed by others such as Pareto, Michels, Mannheim, Burnham, Mills and Keller. In recent decades numerous empirical studies of societal and community elites have been undertaken.[2]

This activity led to the development of a sociological tradition using the concept 'elite', and covering similar ground to work done by writers using concepts such as status, leadership, power, stratification and influence, all of which relate to the same phenomenon, namely the existence of a category of people at the top of status hierarchies. Writers active in the field have formulated definitions according to their respective empirical realities and theoretical perspectives, which has thwarted ideals of terminological consensus.

While it is beyond the scope of this book to redress the problem, to proceed meaningfully with an analysis of the African elite in South Africa one cannot escape some or other definition of the concept 'elite' and the danger of falling into the same trap as previous writers. A way out was found by analysing the content of a number of definitions encountered in the literature and, from that, constructing a working definition. The most common dimensions encountered were power, achieved status, cohesion, minority, function, esteem and privilege – singularly or in combination with each other.

Although divergent in approach and focus, the definitions convey essentially the same content, namely, that largely through their own efforts a minority of individuals fill socially valued positions related to the functioning of society which enable them to exert social power.

It is sufficient for this book to regard the African elite of South Africa as the African incumbents of functionally important positions in various institutional sectors. They gained their elite status through achievement in various sectors and then became opinion-leaders to the broader African community, and in some cases to the wider South African society.

IDENTIFYING ELITES

The three main procedures for the identification of individuals in the elite as described in the literature are the positional approach, the reputational approach and the decision-making approach.

The Positional Approach

The positional approach has its origins in the work of Mills[3] and is the procedure favoured by sociologists working with national samples. Individuals in the elite are identified by the positions they occupy at the top of important national organizations. Criticism of this approach mainly concerns the assumption that all social power is found in organizations while informal power is negated.

The Reputational Approach

The reputational approach is favoured by political scientists working in local communities and has its origins in the work of Hunter.[4] He compiled lists of the influential people in a community by consulting knowledgeable people in that community. He then asked a panel of leaders from different sectors in the community to edit and shorten the list. Finally the people on the list were themselves asked to nominate the forty most important people in the community. Criticism of this procedure lies in the arbitrary nature of the selection of the original informants and the panel, the rationale for the length of the list, and the selection process itself which indicates reputation for power rather than power itself.

The Decision-Making Approach

The decision-making approach has its origins in the work of Dahl,[5] who argued that there is a difference between those with the potential to exercise power and those who do in fact exercise power. Dahl analysed the decision-making process in a community's education system, urban development programme and political nominations to determine the most influential people in that community. The approach was criticized on the grounds that the decisions that lend themselves to such an analysis are esoteric and controversial, while institutionalized decision-making is ignored, the role of manipulation and vested interests is ignored and that political-type decisions are overemphasized.

IDENTIFYING THE MODERN AFRICAN ELITE IN SOUTH AFRICA

General Procedure

The procedure followed in this book was based on the positional approach and supplemented by aspects of the reputational approach. In terms of the positional approach, various institutional sectors had to be identified within which elite positions could be found. At the present stage of integration of the African community into the modern differentiated component of South African society, the sectors within which Africans can advance and consequently within which an African elite could be identified, are business, religion, professions and community life. The polity was one of the sectors that had to be excluded, as the African community does not take part in the institutionalized political process in South Africa and none of the methodological approaches could be relied upon to identify a legitimate political elite. Many of the people identified as members of the elite in the other sectors were also found to be active in politics and performed functions that would otherwise be performed by a political elite.

As each sector is organized differently the procedures used to identify the elite had to be modified to suit each case. The procedures followed are described below. In some instances details are blurred to prevent the identification of personalities.

Sixty people were interviewed – fifteen each from business, religion and professions, and five each from the arts, sport and women's activities as representative of community life.

Business

Although Africans have always been part of the modern economic system as labourers, upward occupational mobility in the business sector has occurred only relatively recently following the removal of formal racial discrimination in industry, the legalization of Black trade unions, changed attitudes of White businessmen and the extension of trading rights to Africans. The people occupying elite positions in business were identified by using the positional and reputational approaches. To achieve representativeness, three subsectors were distinguished in each of which five people were identified to be interviewed. These subsectors are private enterprise, the trade unions, and managers in White-controlled organizations.

A national African chamber of commerce was approached to help with the identification of the most prominent African entrepreneurs. After many discussions with senior officials, a list was compiled based on the size of enterprise, management effectiveness reflected by the winning of awards made by the chamber, and type of operation to avoid more than one person being drawn from the same field. To obtain respondents from the trade unions a list was compiled of the largest trade unions, registered as well as unregistered, and the chief executive officer of each was approached, starting with the largest union, until five interviews were completed. An association of Black managers suggested a list of prominent African managers in White-controlled companies, with due regard to the type of business, to obtain a broad spread of interests. The list was confirmed by enquiries in the business sector and included people not belonging to the association.

Religion

The early activity of missionaries among the African population which led to the inclusion of Africans in formal religious structures at an early stage as well as the reluctance of the government to be seen to interfere in church affairs, has resulted in religion becoming the most differentiated sector in South African society. Religion has consequently presented Africans with the best available opportunity for upward occupational mobility in the modern sector.

The identification of the religious elite began with the listing of denominations with the largest African membership according to the 1980 census. Interviews were conducted with two leaders in each of the churches with 300 000 and more African followers, and interviews with one leader in each of the churches with between 100 000 and 300 000 followers. As churches are organized dissimilarly, a different procedure was followed to select individuals in each church, although the principle followed throughout was the identification of the organizationally most influential position occupied by an African, which was often in any case the most powerful position in a church. Attempts were also made to include different kinds of church activities. For example, where the larger churches, in respect of which two people were required, had a full-time African general secretary, he was included along with the most prominent parish priest. In all cases the priest was either the elected leader of the church assembly or, if he was not African, the priest in the largest congregation (considering members of all races) that had an African priest. In the rare cases that the same denomination was represented by different churches, the church with the greatest number of African followers was included.

Professions

The gradual incorporation of the African community into the modern sector of South African society and the consequent exposure of Africans to a variety of institutional sectors, has resulted in their inclusion in professional structures and advance to the top of professional status systems. Most Africans are, however, still to be found in professions such as teaching and nursing which are associated with the first generation to be educated.

The usual definition of a profession as a functionally specific occupational group with control over the practice of its profession was used to select professions, although African professionals, despite being organized, play little if any role in the control over their profession in South Africa while they still practice in racially segregated environments. The professions represented are medicine, nursing, law, education, journalism and social work, with either two or three interviews conducted in each profession depending on the prominence of that particular profession in the African community. The general procedure followed was to approach the national leader and one of the provincial leaders of the relevant professional organization, or the most senior African in a professional organization if the national organization was led by a White. Attempts were made to include individuals from different fields within each profession. Where the positional approach was inappropriate the reputational approach was used to identify the most prominent person.

Community Life

In modern societies informal institutions provide opportunities for expression that are not otherwise available to people occupying subordinate positions in formal institutions. This is particularly true of the African community which is collectively excluded from the societal community. Three informal sectors that have produced prominent actors in the African community (namely sport, art and women's activities) were consequently included in the sample to provide a wider representation of the African elite. Five successful artists and entertainers from different genres (fiction, sculpture, drama, music and painting), the top administrators of the five largest sports in the African community and five of the most prominent feminist leaders were interviewed. The sports administrators were identified by the positional approach and the artists and feminists by the reputational approach.

The ultimate objective of all the methodological decisions was to interview the people whom any informed analyst would regard as the people at the top of the social hierarchy in the modern African community. The positional and reputational approaches served this purpose admirably. Each respondent was asked about the other people in his field who ought also to be interviewed to test the selection already made. This means that the reputational approach was used more often than is suggested earlier in this chapter. In the end the people interviewed include all the well-known personalities in the African community at the time of the research. They are in some instances publicly better known in spheres other than those for which they were identified.

The information-gathering technique employed was what is commonly known as the structured interview, using a pre-compiled interview guide (see Appendix), although material not provided for in the interview guide was forthcoming and is included in the analysis. In many cases, curricula vitae were obtained from secretaries beforehand to prepare for the interview, which provided additional information that could be used in the analysis. The interviews lasted from fifty minutes to two hours and were conducted from May to August 1985. Interviews took place all over the country. In most cases respondents were visited. Five interviews took place while respondents were in the Transvaal on business. In only three cases could people originally identified not be interviewed. One refused outright ('I really don't see how this can help me with my work'), one was overseas for the duration of the fieldwork, while the third did not conduct interviews of any kind with anyone. There were the usual problems experienced when trying to arrange interviews with busy people. In some cases an interview took place only after a fourth appointment had been made. Once the interview commenced the respondents were very co-operative and ventured more information than was required. They seemed to enjoy talking about themselves. Contrary to advice beforehand that they would not discuss their involvement with traditional practices, many prefaced their answers with 'Whites don't understand this' and proceeded with a detailed explication of tribal customs and how they experience them. The advice that 'they will talk to you about anything except their involvement in politics' was valid, however. When asked whether they belong to a political organization, all declined to answer. In reaction to other questions many inadvertently referred to their active involvement in politics. This was not pursued further.

A final remark must be made about the use of the concept 'elite'. In recent years reservations have been expressed about the use of the word, as its meaning in common parlance is often confused with its sociological meaning. Even its sociological usage is the subject of controversy and it is seen to refer to an ideology of the status quo.[6] At the outset problems were encountered with the use of the term. A typical reaction was the following: 'First the Whites tried to divide us into tribes. Then they spoke of the middle class. Then we were separated into urban and rural Blacks. Now you come with the "elite". We are all one nation and will not be divided.' This problem was resolved by the use of the term 'opinion-leader' in the interviews. 'Opinion-leader', which is coterminous with 'elite' in the literature although not as often used, elicited no comment at all. In the final instance it is the empirical result that must be judged and not the meanings people variously attach to words.

2 Origin and Early Socialization

INTRODUCTION

When industrialization began in South Africa the African population lived in functionally undifferentiated rural settlements. As the national economy developed and diversified, the whole African population was directly or indirectly drawn into it. Thousands of Africans migrated to the urban areas to take up employment as migrant or permanently settled workers, while those that could not or preferred not to live in the cities – notably women (and children) and the elderly – became increasingly dependent on cash remittances from male relatives in town. Urban influences permeated even remote rural areas in the form of urban values and modern consumer goods introduced by returning workers, which changed traditional lifestyles and in turn increased the pressure for urbanization.

For the overwhelming majority of the African population this process of urbanization and involvement in a Western-type society was triggered off by the discovery of diamonds and gold in the last quarter of the nineteenth century. In the early phase of economic diversification the participation of Africans was limited to unskilled occupations in agriculture and mining. When industrial development and diversification gained momentum during and after the Second World War, opportunities arose for upward occupational mobility. At more or less the same time the National Party came to power, and its policy of apartheid, later called separate development, legalized the social and economic colour bar that had evolved over time, which in turn severely limited opportunities for the upward mobility of Africans. Towards the end of the 1970s a process of reconstitution of societal structures began to eliminate these constraints, and as time went by more and more Africans advanced in the various sectors of the modern Westernized economy. Until these opportunities became available to Africans their occupational advancement was largely limited to those professions in which they could serve their own community, such as religion and education. It is against this background of the social evolution of South Africa that the socialization of the elite took place.

15

GENDER AND AGE

Elites in the modern African community appear to be predominantly male. Of the sixty people that were identified as elite for this study only ten turned out to be women. If the five women that were specifically included as representatives of women's activities are disregarded, then only five of some fifty-five were found to be women. This complies with the situation in the rest of the African community where women are not often found in leadership roles. According to Table 2.1, African women are underrepresented in professions other than nursing and teaching which are generally considered to be traditionally female occupations, while there are very few of them in the managerial, administrative and executive occupational category.

The experience of other modern societies shows that women achieve elite status very late. Even of a society as differentiated as America it has been said that women are seriously under-represented at the top of the institutional structure.[1] Among White South Africans as well as in Norway women were found to comprise only 3 per cent of the elite and in Australia only 1 per cent.[2,3]

Table 2.1   Comparison of the number of African and White women and men in selected professions and occupational groups, RSA, 1983

	Women		Men	
	African	White	African	White
Profession				
Doctor/dentist	39	1 512	225	16 096
Medical/dental technician	50	1 062	142	870
University/college lecturer	329	3 371	554	8 794
Law	40	592	214	6 055
Public relations	19	795	136	989
Programmer/systems analyst	14	2 207	98	5 585
School teachers	59 279	44 390	30 237	20 302
Nurses and midwives	21 888	21 578	1 108	857
Occupational category				
Professions	95 251	112 958	44 906	201 798
Managerial/admin./ executive	751	22 646	2 109	147 845

Source: Extracted from Prekel, 1986.

The general lack of skills among African women was referred to by women members of the elite when they were interviewed. Those active in voluntary community organizations referred to basic skills – for example:

> Women's literacy is a problem. This makes the task of leadership more difficult. The standard of their literacy and book skills is so low that it is difficult to properly conduct committee meetings.

and:

> Administration-wise it is very difficult to have women in office. They are too emotional and can't get their priorities right. They can't separate local, provincial and national matters. The committees are too own-interested. I can't even find a secretary to handle the clerical work.

Among professionally trained women the lack of leadership qualities also creates problems. For example:

> There is a lack of willingness in Black nurses to come out with their own opinions. They are too subordinate – they don't challenge leadership. There is not enough leadership, independent problem-solving and initiative.

There was evidence that traditional African custom which requires women to be unconditionally subordinate to authority still plays a role in their modern career environment:

> Black women in most areas are still bogged down by traditional laws which stifle their progress. They are victims of traditional and racial oppression. It is much more difficult for them to rise above it.

There was, however, no indication that the female members of the elite had themselves felt any debilitating sexual discrimination. They were obviously strong enough to transcend constraints of that nature, as was indicated by the following example of their reaction to this issue:

> I just threw myself in and did what had to be done without any hang-ups about being a woman.

Table 2.2   Age distribution of the elite

Age in years	Men		Women		Total	
	%	(N)	%	(N)	%	(N)
20–29	2.0	(1)	–		1.7	(1)
30–39	20.0	(10)	–		16.7	(10)
40–49	30.0	(15)	20.0	(2)	28.3	(17)
50–59	34.0	(17)	70.0	(7)	40.0	(24)
60–69	14.0	(7)	10.0	(1)	13.3	(8)
Total	100.0	(50)	100.0	(10)	100.0	(60)

When one looks at the age distribution of the elite, presented in Table 2.2, it seems also that the women tended to be older than the men. Eighty per cent of the women were older than fifty, compared with 48 per cent of the men.

It was to be expected that the elite would be of a fairly advanced age, as elite status is an achieved status. Elites in other societies are often reported to be in their sixties.[4] The elite in the business sector and the arts tended to be younger than in the other sectors, with 60 per cent of them younger than fifty. The youthfulness of the business elite complies with the history of African involvement in the modern economic sector of South African society, as opportunities for Africans to participate in the business sector have only recently become available. On the other hand, achievement in art is based on talent which is less age-bound than achievement in other sectors.

GEOGRAPHICAL BACKGROUND

There is a strong urban bias among the elite. As is evident from Table 2.3, 80 per cent (48) of them live in a metropolitan area while 56.7 per cent (34) grew up in a metropolitan area. This reflects a higher rate of urbanization than that of the total African population. In 1980 only 43.44 per cent of the Black population outside the homelands lived in one of the metropolitan areas.[5,6] The strength of the urban bias in the background of the elite becomes more evident when age is taken into consideration. In 1936, i.e. more or less at the time of birth of most of the elite, only 17.3 per cent of the African population of South Africa lived in urban areas.[7] In other parts of the world elites also tend to be city dwellers.[8]

When these figures are put into a generational perspective, as is

Table 2.3   Domicilium of the elite in childhood and adulthood

Domicilium	Men		Women		Total	
	Child-hood % (N)	Adult-hood % (N)	Child-hood % (N)	Adult-hood % (N)	Child-hood % (N)	Adult-hood % (N)
Rural	38.0 (19)	–	10.0 (1)	–	33.3 (20)	–
Town	12.0 (6)	22.0 (11)	–	10.0 (1)	10.0 (6)	20.0 (12)
Metropolitan	50.0 (25)	78.0 (39)	90.0 (9)	90.0 (9)	56.7 (34)	80.0 (48)
Total	100.0 (50)	100.0 (50)	100.0 (10)	100.0 (10)	100.0 (60)	100.0 (60)

Table 2.4   Domicilium of the elite and two preceding generations

Domicilium	Generation					
	Elite		Mother		Grandfather	
	%	(N)	%	(N)	%	(N)
Rural	–		36.7	(22)	82.8	(48)
Town	20.0	(12)	10.0	(6)	6.9	(4)
Metropolitan	80.0	(48)	53.3	(32)	10.3	(6)
Total	100.0	(60)	100.0	(60)	100.0	(58)*

* The domicilium of two grandfathers is unknown.

done in Table 2.4, it is evident that the general migration of Africans to the urban areas also occurred in the families of the elite. All of the elite live in an urban environment, compared with 63.3 per cent (38) of their mothers and 17.2 per cent (10) of their grandfathers. Because of the system of migrant labour it is difficult to categorize the domicilium of their fathers.

Another way of looking at the urbanism of the elite is to analyse the number of them that belong to the first, second or third generation in their family to live in a city. This is done in Table 2.5, from which it is evident that a city domicilium rarely went back as far as the third generation.

In most cases (70 per cent, or 42) the elite grew up in complete families where both parents were present. Ten per cent (6) lost their father while they were very young while 6.7 per cent (4) grew up in broken homes with their parents either divorced or separated. Ten per cent (6) of the elite seldom saw their father, as he had been a migrant worker spending most of the year away at work, while 3.3

Table 2.5   City generations reflected in the elite

City generation	Men		Women		Total	
	%	(N)	%	(N)	%	(N)
First	45.7	(21)	12.5	(1)	40.7	(22)
Second	45.7	(21)	62.5	(5)	48.1	(26)
Third	8.7	(4)	25.0	(2)	11.1	(6)
Total	100.0	(46)	100.0	(8)	100.0	(54)*

* Excludes those that have never lived in a city but includes those who have a city background and are now living in a town to practise their profession.

per cent (2) had been sent to school away from home. Most of the elite described their parental home as having a beneficial effect on their socialization. For example:

> In terms of important values the most important influence came from my parents. They were good examples. They were simple people but I haven't reached their level yet.

Others described their parental home as a refuge from a hostile environment:

> I come from a very conservative Catholic family. I was born in a very ravaged and deprived neighbourhood where survival was critical at an early age. My parents had no education so they became sticklers for education. Our parents protected us from bad influences in the neighbourhood. We were not allowed to go to movies and we had to be home before dark. We had to go to church. These early learning experiences made me determined to fight on. I am basically a fighter.

Although they often were poor, the elite grew up in cohesive families from where they could concentrate on developing their potential.

SCHOOL EDUCATION

School education played an important part in the socialization of the elite. Most of them referred to happy experiences at school. As is

Table 2.6 Type of school attended by the elite

School type	Men		Women		Total	
	%	(N)	%	(N)	%	(N)
Farm	2.0	(1)	–		1.7	(1)
Government	36.0	(18)	40.0	(4)	36.7	(22)
Mission	62.0	(31)	60.0	(6)	61.7	(37)
Total	100.0	(50)	100.0	(10)	100.0	(60)

reflected by Table 2.6, more than half, namely 61.7 per cent (37), went to mission schools.

As opportunities for a mission-school education ended with the implementation of the Bantu Education Act (no. 47 of 1953) and consequent government control over all African education, it is mainly those that are older than forty that were able to attend mission schools. This means that the older members of the elite were of the last generation to receive a mission-school education, which was generally thought to provide a better education than government schools. It was the aim of Bantu education to prepare Africans to serve their community in the traditional areas and not for inclusion in the modern Westernized economy, as was explained by the then minister of native affairs:

> By simply blindly producing pupils who were trained in European ideas the idle hope was created that they could occupy positions in the European community in spite of the country's policy . . . This is what is meant by the unhealthy creation of white-collar ideals and the creation of widespread frustration among the so-called educated natives . . . The school education must equip him to meet the demands which the economic life in South Africa will make on him.[9]

In a public statement on 2 May 1986, the minister responsible for African education said that this policy has since been abandoned and that education must prepare Africans for 'the common reality of the modern industrialized and urbanized environment with its strong Western influence'.[10]

The mission schools the elite attended were those that became famous for their alumni, such as the Lovedale Institution at Alice, Adams College and Inanda Seminary in Durban, Marianhill near

Pietermaritzburg, Botshabelo near Middelburg in the Transvaal, Kilnerton Institution in Pretoria, Wilberforce College at Evaton and Pax College near Pietersburg. A strong attendance at private, select schools is also widely found in societies as disparate as those of America, the Philippines and Tanzania, although not in the case of White South African elites.[11] These schools were conduits of Western social values that induced their pupils to achieve, as a woman in the elite suggested:

> I went to Inanda Seminary to do Form 1. I was about thirteen years old. During the first week I admired a teacher, Miss Levina Scott. I was on the lookout for the headmaster to see what he was like. Then I found she ran the school. I felt that if she can run a school, why can't I. The sky is the limit. So I aimed high and I kept it that way.

A man referred to his schooling as follows:

> My father has a very strong influence on me. Then the superintendent minister of my church, the late Bishop Pakendorf. At Kilnerton Institution, the principal Dr Ken Hartshorne – I loved him. A Black teacher at Botshabelo introduced me to the love of history and cultural things.

The government of the time was criticized for the Bantu Education policy and the effect that it was expected to have on the African community. Many of the elite that had planned to become teachers turned away from the profession as a result. For example:

> I felt I wanted to be a teacher to be in contact with young people. But I was discouraged by the introduction of Bantu Education so I did typing, shorthand and bookkeeping. I just loved playing with groups of children as a child.

In general the elite were a privileged group in the opportunities they enjoyed to attend school. They all attended school, many of them the superior mission schools, while even in 1980 only 56.2 per cent of the African population of school-going age (6–19 years) were at school.[12] More than two-thirds of the elite, namely 68.3 per cent (41), were able to attend school full time until they had completed std. 10. The educational level they attained is presented in Table 2.7.

Table 2.7 Educational level of the elite

Education	Men		Women		Total	
	%	(N)	%	(N)	%	(N)
Std. 6	2.0	(1)	–		1.7	(1)
Std. 8	6.0	(3)	10.0	(1)	6.7	(4)
Std. 9	2.0	(1)	10.0	(1)	3.3	(2)
Std. 10	6.0	(3)	–		5.0	(3)
Std. 8/9+Diploma	8.0	(4)	–		6.7	(4)
Std. 10+Diploma	10.0	(5)	10.0	(1)	10.0	(6)
1 Degree	12.0	(6)	20.0	(2)	13.3	(8)
2 Degrees/diploma*	18.0	(9)	10.0	(1)	16.7	(10)
3 Degrees/diploma*	36.0	(18)	40.0	(4)	36.7	(22)
Total	100.0	(50)	100.0	(10)	100.0	(60)

*Post-graduate university diplomas for which a degree is a prerequisite.

A total of 76.7 per cent (46) of the elite went on to obtain further academic qualifications after std. 10, while 6.7 per cent (4) obtained further occupational training after std. 8 or std. 9. Their further training is discussed more fully later in this chapter.

The conditions under which the elite obtained their schooling is evident from their recollections of their schooldays. Some went to live with relatives who paid for their schooling while others were promising scholars whom teachers took into their homes. Furthermore most of the mission schools accepted promising children who were not able to make any contribution to the cost of their schooling. This is similar to the experience of tropical Africa, where children from illiterate homes were frequently the only children from a rural area to attain elite status as they were recognised by the local missionary to be bright and were helped towards scholarships.[13]

The importance that the families of the elite attached to the education of promising children and the means by which they attained their education in spite of poverty, is exemplified by this man's history:

My parents were so poor that they couldn't put me through education. I went to a school run by the Lutheran Church. They wouldn't let anyone leave the village until they were confirmed. I passed std. 7 which was as far as the school went but because I wasn't yet confirmed I had to stay at school. I repeated std. 7 and then they used me as a teacher. My brother was working as a domestic servant in Pretoria. He sent me ten shillings for the busfare to Middelburg to look for a job to earn money to make it to Pretoria. In Middelburg a woman who later turned out to be an aunt of mine recognised me in the street and took me to the Botshabelo mission. It was a teacher training centre. A cousin was studying there. He took me to the governer of the college. I was there for three years and got a teacher's diploma. A teacher took an interest in me and persuaded me to get a junior certificate so that I could earn one pound more a month as a teacher. I then stayed for matric which would have earned me two pounds more a month. My brother knew people at [the University of] Fort Hare who told him that if I had matric I could get a bursary for Fort Hare. So I went there.

PARENTS' AND GRANDFATHERS' EDUCATION AND OCCUPATION

Although the fathers of the elite were a little better educated than their mothers, who in turn had higher educational qualifications than their grandfathers, there was a general scarcity of education in the generations preceding the elite, as is reflected in Table 2.8. More than half, namely 61.8 per cent (34) of the 55 fathers whose education is known, had less schooling than std. 6. Most of the parents who had had no formal schooling nevertheless learnt to read and write under the guidance of missionaries. Although the parents of the elite had little formal education, they were, generally speaking, better educated than even the 1980 African population. In comparison, 55 per cent of the fathers of White South African elites completed their schooling,[14] while in other modern societies, for example Australia,[15] fathers often held degrees.

The educational advantage of their parents over the African community provided the elite with an environment conducive to study, as a man suggested:

I've had good people helping me. I inherited qualities from my parents such as native intelligence. My father was reasonably well-educated. I enjoyed an environment that was not too common at the time. It gave me a head start. I liked reading because of the books at home. My father was smart – he also let us read comics. I got my greed for reading from comics.

Table 2.8 Highest educational level of the elite compared to that of their parents, paternal grandfather and the RSA 1980 African population over the age of 25

Education	Elite %	Elite (N)	Father %	Father (N)	Mother %	Mother (N)	G/father %	G/father (N)	Africans RSA 1980† %
Unknown	—		8.3	(5)	1.7	(1)	53.3	(32)	1.14
None	—		18.3	(11)	23.3	(14)	36.7	(22)	43.49
Up to Std 5	—		38.3	(23)	58.3	(35)	5.0	(3)	35.30
Std 6–8	8.3	(5)	6.7	(4)	3.3	(2)	1.7	(1)	16.99
Std 9	3.3	(2)	1.7	(1)	—		—		0.86
Std 10	5.0	(3)	10.0	(6)	3.3	(2)	—		1.10
Std 9+Dipl	6.7	(4)*	10.0	(6)*	8.3	(5)*	3.3	(2)*	0.60
Std 10+Dipl	10.0	(6)	5.0	(3)	1.7	(1)	—		0.38
Degree	66.7	(40)	1.7	(1)	—		—		0.10
Total	100.0	(60)	100.0	(60)	100.0	(60)	100.0	(60)	100.00

* Includes Std 8+Diploma.
†*Source*: Calculated from RSA Population Census 1980, Report 02–80–12.

Table 2.9 The post-school educated elite in generational perspective

Educated generation	Men %	Men (N)	Women %	Women (N)	Total %	Total (N)
First	69.0	(29)	37.5	(3)	34.0	(32)
Second	26.2	(11)	50.0	(4)	30.0	(15)
Third	4.8	(2)	12.5	(1)	6.0	(3)
Total	100.0	(42)	100.0	(8)	100.0	(50)*

* Ten had no training beyond school.

Table 2.9 presents the generational perspective on the post-school (including post-std. 8 and post-std. 9) education of the elite in a more simplified form. It is evident from the table that the men were mostly of the first generation in their family to be educated beyond school while the women were mainly of the second educated generation. Although the figures are small they comply with the tendency in other societies to give educational opportunities to sons first.[16]

The sector with the best-educated fathers, that is, fathers with a std. 10 certificate or higher, were the feminists (60 per cent, or 30) followed by the professionals (37.5 per cent, or 5). Only 28.6 per cent

(4) of the religious elite, 21.4 per cent (3) of the business elite, 20 per cent (1) of the artists and none of the sports administrators had fathers who completed their schooling. These figures reflect the tendency also found in other societies for professional people to come from the higher-educated families, while feminists tend to come from families in the higher socio-economic levels that have been freed from an existence of mundane household routine.[17]

Only six of the twenty-eight grandfathers whose education is known, had any schooling at all. It does not seem likely that those whose education and occupation are unknown had any education whatsoever, as it would have been noted as unusual, and remembered.

As the elite grew up in an era when formal education in the parental generation was scarce, skills acquired in other occupations gave their parents an advantage from which they could encourage their children to study. This was exemplified by a man in describing the people who had played a beneficial role in his socialization:

> First my father who has never been to school. He was successful in life but had no formal education. Through Bible school he learnt to read and write and became a leader there. Then there was the Rev. Dlamini who was also not educated. So I have been challenged by people who have never been educated.

A woman told of the methods her father, a teacher, had used to encourage her to study:

> My father used to encourage us by telling stories about poor people. One I remember was about a very poor woman whose children nagged her for food. She didn't have any money to buy food so she washed her only dress and applied for a job. She stood in a long queue for the interview among other well-dressed people. When she got into the interview she felt the man's hostility at her poverty. When she presented him with a yellowed and tattered piece of paper he appointed her immediately and asked when she could start. What was on the piece of paper? Her educational qualification!

In addition to their educational advantage, the parents of the elite also occupied higher-rated occupations. From Table 2.10 it is evident that more than half of the fathers practised skilled occupations. As many as 15 per cent of their paternal grandfathers were in skilled

Table 2.10   Occupations of the mothers, fathers and paternal grandfathers
of the elite

Occupation	Mother % (N)		Father % (N)		Grandfather % (N)	
Skilled:						
Teacher	10.0	(6)	16.7	(10)	1.7	(1)
Own business	5.0	(3)	8.3	(5)	–	
Minister/evangelist	–		11.7	(7)	10.0	(6)
Chef	–		3.3	(2)	–	
Driver/artisan	–		8.3	(5)	1.7	(1)
Clerk	–		6.7	(4)	–	
Welfare officer	–		1.7	(1)	–	
Policeman	–		1.7	(1)	1.7	(1)
Sub-total	15.0	(9)	58.3	(35)	15.0	(9)
Unskilled:						
Labourer	5.0	(3)	31.7	(19)	15.0	(9)
Domestic servant	35.0	(21)	–		–	
Housewife	45.0	(27)	–		–	
Traditional farmer	–		5.0	(3)	31.7	(19)
Tribal chief	–		1.7	(1)	13.3	(8)
Sub-total	85.0	(51)	38.3	(23)	60.0	(36)
Unknown	–		3.3	(2)	25.0	(15)
Total	100.0	(60)	100.0	(60)	100.0	(60)

occupations. When the grandfathers that were tribal chiefs is added
to this, it means that almost half of the grandfathers were in high-
status occupations.

Similar findings, namely that the fathers of the elite practise
trained occupations – often intellectual professions as teachers and
clergymen – in the middle class, while mothers are at least literate,
have been reported from a wide variety of other societies.[18] In West
Africa many members of the elite were found to come from families
highly placed in traditional status hierachies. However, as elite
recruitment is open in the sense that it is an achieved status, lower-
caste people have been recruited into the elite on the basis of their
educational achievements, albeit not in absolute proportion to their
numbers.[19] In Tanzania it was found that although the elite grew up
in rural areas where three-quarters of them herded cattle or goats as
children, their families were of above-average wealth in their
community.[20] It is generally known that children with higher class
origins are more likely to aspire to high educational and occupational

goals than are children of lower social class origins.[21] It was noticed of Transkei elites that the children of upper-class people were persisters in the school system, getting further than children from ordinary families.[22]

It is quite obvious that the parents of the elite in this study were highly placed in the African stratification system of their generation. Signs of upward occupational mobility were common while achievement-orientated values were also found to be present among their grandfathers. For example:

> I was possibly a little luckier. My granddad was a hard worker and he saved a little to send his son, my uncle, to school. He became an inspiration to the whole family. He encouraged me to learn and I went to live with him in Brakpan where he taught at a school.

Evidence of a socialization in terms of Western achievement-orientated values emerged many times, as is exemplified by the following:

> It was a matter of luck. I come from an educated family. My father was a teacher and a minister in the Lutheran Church while he had his own farm. He educated us. I was born into a family in which we had to succeed. It was an above-average family. I had the chances.

Women were just as often encouraged as men, as a woman indicated when she referred to her father:

> He was someone who recognised my potential and encouraged me. He was a leader in the community as a civil leader. He called me for discussions and tested his ideas on me.

POST-SCHOOL EDUCATION OF THE ELITE

When one considers the supportive role of their parents notwithstanding their socio-economic circumstances, it is perhaps not surprising that the elite became as educated as they did. As is evident from Table 2.11, 76.7 per cent (46) of them held one or more degrees or diplomas after completing std. 10, compared with the 17.94 per cent of the 1980 White population.

The high number of degrees among elites, especially post-graduate

Table 2.11 Post-school education of the elite compared to the 1980 RSA
White population older than 25

Education	Elite % (N)	RSA Whites[†] %
N.a:None/Unknown	–	3.55
N.a:Only school	16.7 (10)	76.29
Std. 9+Diploma	6.7 (4)*	2.23
Std. 10+Diploma	10.0 (6)	11.10
B-degree	38.3 (23)	5.98
M-degree	20.0 (12)	0.60
D-degree	8.3 (5)	0.26
Total	100.0 (60)	100.0

* Includes Std 8+Diploma.
[†]*Source*: Calculated from Population Census 1980, Report 02-80-12.

degrees – in some cases more than half the members of elites have
higher degrees – has also been found in a variety of other societies.[23]

A total of 28.3 per cent (17) of the elite attained one or more of
their degrees at universities overseas. In addition, 3.3 per cent (2)
had been awarded one or more honorary doctorates by universities
overseas, while another 1.7 per cent (1) had been awarded an
honorary doctorate by a South African city university. The value of
attendance at universities overseas was described as follows:

> I was lucky with an overseas education in a healthy atmosphere
> where I was challenged to give of my best and still know that many
> others are better. I was lucky to be educated in a cosmopolitan
> atmosphere which freed me from an anti-White feeling and gave
> me a positive outlook. People I've worked with from all population
> groups have remarked that they do not feel threatened.

The elite that represent the first generation to live in a city were the
best educated. A total of 90.9 per cent (20) of the first generation to
live in a city had post-school qualifications, while 81.8 per cent (18) of
them had one or more degrees. Among the second generation to live
in a city, 80.8 per cent (21) had post-school qualifications and 57.7
per cent (15) one or more degrees. Of the third generation, 66.7 per
cent (4) had post-school qualifications in the form of degrees. This

may be explained by the supposition that the most promising scholars were helped to continue their education and then migrated to the cities or, conversely, that those wanting to migrate to the cities saw higher education as a means to obtain urban rights,[24] as is exemplified by a man who grew up in a rural area:

> I can't tell you how many [times] the West-Rand Administration Board stamped by book '72 hours'. I went back and said, 'No, I can't eat.' I wanted city rights and I needed a university degree for it. Books and learning are in the city and I needed to go there. At school I thought teaching was best. I tried BA but wasn't interested. I rubbed shoulders with influx control and decided to fight it by studying law. I was always motivated to fight injustice. I always wanted to better my life. The best place to read and improve my quality of life is in the urban areas. My interests are in urban areas.

Fifteen per cent (9) of the elite mentioned that in addition to their formal academic qualifications, they had received informal training later in their career by attending courses such as those in management and labour relations.

Most of the elite that went to university obtained financial assistance to attend a residential university. Of the 49 (81.7 per cent) of the elite that had studied, 77.6 per cent (38) obtained their first post-school qualification by full-time attendance at a university or college, while 22.4 per cent (11) obtained theirs by part-time study. More men (80.5 per cent, or 33) enjoyed full-time study than did women (62.5 per cent, or 5).

FAMILY CONSTELLATION

The elite are all products of the conjugal family system. They were members of families with an average of 6.5 children (median 6). Only 3.3 per cent (2) were only children, while 3.3 per cent (2) grew up in families with 14 children. The men grew up in slightly larger families (average number of children 6.8) than the women (average number of children 5.1).

The well-known effect of education on family size is evident when the size of the families the elite grew up in is analysed. Those that had no education beyond school grew up in families with an average of 7.2 children, those that are the first generation in their families to be educated grew up in families with 6.6 children, while the second educated generation grew up in families with 6.1 children, and the third educated generation in families with 4.7 children.

The well-known relationship between geographical background and family size was also confirmed. Those that grew up in a rural area came from families with an average of 6.8 children, compared with the family size of 6.2 children in respect of those that grew up in towns and 6.4 children in respect of those that grew up in cities. Put another way, the first generation to live in a city grew up in families with 6.9 children, the second generation in families with 6.3 children, and the third generation in families with an average of 6.2 children.

When one looks at the birth order of the elite, it is evident that most of them (55 per cent, or 33) were one of the middle children in their family, while 30 per cent (18) were eldest children and 11.7 per cent (7) youngest children. A total of 3.3 per cent (2) were only children.

Although they did not enjoy comparing themselves with their own relatives, most of the elite (73.3 per cent, or 44) considered themselves to have attained a higher social status than their siblings, while 21.7 per cent (13) thought their status was similar. No one mentioned siblings with a higher status than himself. Slightly more women (70 per cent, or 7) than men (61.7 per cent, or 37) said that their status was the highest in their family. There were two brothers in the elite – professionals in different fields.

INFLUENCES

The social background of the elite indicates that they were socialized in modern, non-traditional values and that they internalized achievement-oriented values at an early age. Although other aspects came to the fore, as is shown in Table 2.12, they considered their home and school environment to have been the most formative.

The elite's emphasis on the role of their parents confirms evidence from the literature that there is a strong relationship between home environment and the need to achieve. The socializing factors that have been identified in the need to achieve are warm and loving parents that set high levels of aspiration for their children, even as toddlers in respect of household chores. Mothers were found to be independent, strong-willed people, while fathers were softer and less domineering, which results in their children developing initiative and

Table 2.12　Early influences in the socialization of the elite

Influences	%	(N)
Outstanding/encouraging parents	38.3	(23)
School principals/teachers	35.0	(21)
White SA personalities	21.7	(13)
Black SA personalities	18.3	(11)
A supportive family	13.3	(8)
Christian family background	11.7	(7)
Relatives outside their nuclear family	10.0	(6)
Minister/evangelist	6.7	(4)
Struggling/poor family background	3.3	(2)
The Black struggle	3.3	(2)
Foreign Black personalities	3.3	(2)
N.a: Did his/her own thing	21.7	(13)

self-reliance.[25] The role of parents and particularly fathers in the socialization of the elite has been referred to many times in the preceding sections. That the elite also recognised the role of their mothers is evident from the following:

> My background of a very Christian family. My father had tremendous influence. He was a great churchman and leader who would have gone far with education. My mother was also a great leader with her example and guidance. She was fairly well educated for those days, with a std. 5. She was president of the African church women's association without even being a minister's wife.

and:

> Always my mother. She planted faith in me by working hard. She always had an encouraging face. She was always hopeful and always found something positive in what happened.

An interesting influence was that of other relatives who sometimes took the place of absent parents. This is probably a continuation of the family support system that existed in the extended family of the traditional African environment, and was referred to a few times – for example:

> My uncle. I grew up with him and he didn't allow me to play with

other boys. After school I had to work in his studio. My company was the radio, and his friends – intelligentsia which gave me exposure and sophistication I wouldn't otherwise have had. Then there was a teacher who is now out of the country who persuaded my uncle not to take me out of school. My mother was also very determined. Her parents were well-off but she refused to take help from them.

and:

My father was a sickly man. He never kept a job. He was illiterate. My mother was a lay teacher and a big influence. She was always sewing and didn't have much time for me. My aunt brought me up. She used to talk a lot about my grandfather and the early Zulu history. She really stimulated me.

Many of the elite were influenced by school-teachers and people prominent at the time they were growing up. The most often mentioned South African personalities were the nationalist leader Nelson Mandela, academic and nationalist leader Professor Z. K. Matthews, and the Anglican priest Trevor Huddleston. Others mentioned more than once were Oliver Tambo, Albert Luthuli, Manas Buthelezi, Can Themba, Richard Gugushe, Carl Mokgokong, Ellen Hellman, Monica Wilson and Ken Hartshorne. This influence was described as follows:

Two people steered me. Nelson Mandela and Oliver Tambo who were in a law partnership. I read about them as I was growing up. I went to court to see them. I was inspired by their dignity and the respect court officials gave them.

and:

My father was an absolute fanatic for achievement, self-assertion and perfection. He was sharp and critical. The pathfinders of Black lawyers like Duma Nokwe who was the first Black advocate, Mandela because of his dignity, stature and humanity, and Godfrey Pitje. From childhood there was only one profession for me that could challenge the system and challenge Whites with their own laws. I do many political cases.

Whites who worked closely with Africans also became role models.
For example:

> My mother who was uneducated beyond primary school. She was a
> very gentle person and a comforter of the afflicted. She had a
> concern for the underdog. Then Father Trevor Huddleston be-
> cause of his compassion. I was in hospital for twenty months with
> TB. He visited me every week. I was struck by his compassion.
> Black teachers in high school gave me a love of English. The present
> principal of Turfloop, Professor Mokgokong, was one of them.

and:

> My role model was my school principal. He has an MA now. He
> encouraged me and also helped me financially. Some White people
> like Kentridge and Chaskalson. I model myself on White people
> like that these days.

They also found Black role models outside the country:

> The late Archbishop Kiwanuka of Uganda who was the first Black
> bishop of modern times. When he was appointed the Pope said to
> him the appointment of future Black bishops depended on whether
> he was a success or failure. In fact he was a great success. I admired
> his vision which made him send people for serious university and
> tertiary education, so that when independence came there was a
> good number of people trained and others had to appeal to them
> for assistance. The second person was the late Archbishop Ma-
> bathoana of Lesotho. He was a kind and affable person who won
> the esteem of many people, White and Black, rich and poor,
> officials and simple people. I appreciated especially the love and
> confidence he inspired, giving free vent to his subordinates to give
> of their best, so that many initiatives were taken by them with an
> occasional word of encouragement on his part.

and:

> My parents. Missionaries. Father Trevor Huddleston, the Angli-
> can priest in Sophiatown. Pax College influenced a lot of things I
> came to admire later on in life, for example, classical music. My

family and Christian traditions and unbringing. Later on people like Martin Luther King had a great influence on me.

Besides personalities, events also led the elite into new careers in which they excelled. For example:

As a child there was a Mr Mohlelegi who was a teacher. Mrs Dival who was a teacher at Kilnerton instilled the love of teaching in me. Then Mr Motsepi, the principal at Kilnerton as well as the principals of the two schools where I taught. I had first wanted to be lawyer. Nelson Mandela and his law firm impressed young peole like myself. I wanted to be in an independent profession. I passed my first-year legal studies. Then the police raided me and found my first-year Unisa notes. They told me I wanted to defend terrorists. I was detained for eight months in terms of the laws regarding unlawful organizations and the suppression of communism. They also tried sabotage but couldn't make it stick. Then while I was on the [Robben] Island I got a calling to the ministry.

The low level of socio-economic conditions in the general African population as well as racial discrimination were other forces for achievement. For example:

Nothing more than the background of tribulations suffered by the Black community is needed to motivate one to work hard for the Black people.

and

The motivating force in my life is to prove that Blacks are not stupid and lousy. I tell young people to strive for excellence in whatever they are doing.

African women, in company with Black women in other multiracial societies, are often said to be disadvantaged by a double set of circumstances – by sexual discrimination in a community in which traditional sex roles are still the norm, while experiencing racial discrimination with the rest of the African community.[26] In the case of the elite this also became a force for achievement, as is evident from the following:

Determination as a Black woman that I should make the grade. I wanted to throw off traditional bonds. I had a pride as a Black woman to watch White women. My mother was a woman and struggled. I set out not to disappoint her.

The need to achieve has been defined as the desire to do well not so much for the sake of social recognition or prestige but to attain an inner feeling of personal accomplishment.[27] It is obvious from the previous sections and confirmed by their own evaluation of their socialization that the elite experienced this need to achieve. Although many were able to mention formative factors, no one can satisfactorily explain his own socialization. A third of the elite did not try to do so. They attributed their success solely to their own efforts and, as is evident from the following quotations, a sense of personal accomplishment was very strong:

There is nothing that beats determination. I'm highly allergic to failure. There is nothing that annoys me like failure. Very few things are impossible. Once I set out for something I get it. Experience is acquired. You are not born with it. Perseverance and determination lead to success. You'll find all African businessmen are self-made men. No one has inherited money. We are all from the school of hard knocks.

and

If I decide to do something I persist with perseverance and discipline. I never postpone things. If I decide to do something I just venture out and do it. I never count the costs. I have never failed in anything. The Lord had helped me. My discipline needed foreign languages. I did them in spite of people telling me I couldn't.

CONCLUSION

As a category of people the elite grew up in conjugal families that had discarded the traditional African way of life and adopted important aspects of the Western value system. Their parents were better educated and practised higher occupations than the rest of the African population, although they were still very far behind the levels achieved by the White population. Because of their family background the elite internalized Western achievement-oriented values. During their early socialization this manifested in a thrust for education, and more than three-quarters of them attained a unversity education, which is much higher than the level of the general White population. Their socialization also enabled them to transcend the general constraints on the upward mobility of Africans which existed in South African society at the time, and put them in a favourable position to utilize the occupational opportunites that come their way.

3 Career

INTRODUCTION

The career development of the elite described in this study took place within a framework of weakening constraints on the upward social mobility of Africans in South Africa. These constraints include poverty, a low level of exposure to Western achievement-orientated values, limited educational opportunities and institutionalized racial discrimination. The effect of these constraints and the extent to which they have weakened over time is evident from Tables 3.1 and 3.2.

Although the African population has advanced both educationally and occupationally over the last quarter century it is still well behind the White population.

The elite transcended these constraints and advanced to the top of status systems in a variety of institutional sectors. The processes involved in their educational advancement were discussed in the previous chapter. In this chapter the attention is focused on their career development as well as aspects of their working environment that shed light on their participation in the modern economy.

Table 3.1 Educational level of the RSA African and White male population over the age of seven years in 1960, 1970 and 1980

Education	Africans			Whites		
	1960 %	*1970* %	*1980* %	*1960* %	*1970* %	*1980* %
None/unknown	60.1	45.9	33.2	3.5	1.0	3.7
Up to std. 5	33.7	44.4	48.3	23.4	20.8	17.3
Std. 6 + 7	4.5	7.0	11.5	30.3	24.0	16.8
Std. 8 + 9	1.1	2.0	5.1	19.2	24.1	23.0
Std. 10	0.1	0.3	1.3	12.2	19.2	23.2
Std. 10+Diploma	0.4	0.3	0.5	7.4	6.3	9.5
Degree	0.0	0.0	0.1	4.0	4.6	6.5
Total	100.0	100.0	100.0	100.0	100.0	100.0

Source: RSA, Presidentsraad 1/1983, table 2.8.

Table 3.2 Occupational sectors represented in the RSA African and White communities in 1960, 1970 and 1980

Occupational sector	Africans			Whites		
	1960 %	1970 %	1980 %	1960 %	1970 %	1980 %
Professional, technical and related	1.25	1.61	3.40	11.98	15.41	19.84
Administrative and managerial	0.15	0.04	0.09	5.12	5.35	7.28
Clerical and related	0.50	1.67	3.70	24.02	26.67	26.97
Sales	0.74	1.38	3.00	8.48	10.35	9.76
Service	18.28	17.81	19.81	5.12	6.81	7.89
Farming, forestry and fishing	37.92	40.37	20.08	10.20	6.36	4.82
Mining, production and transport	33.83	30.64	38.44	32.65	26.10	21.88
Not classifiable	7.34	6.47	11.48	2.44	2.95	1.57
Total economically active	100.00	100.00	100.00	100.00	100.00	100.00

Source: RSA, *Central Statistical Services*, vol. 20, no. 3, Sept. 1986.

CAREER DEVELOPMENT

Because of their high level of education (described in Chapter 2), most of the elite were able to start their working career in a professional post, as is reflected in Table 3.3.

Approximately half of the elite had not changed careers but were still in their first occupation (Table 3.4). Most of the others used the educational and employment opportunities that were available at the time to enter the economic system. Many of the elite used the financial rewards of their first occupation to train for another. Those that had not changed occupation were people who followed careers of their own choice.

A total of 35 per cent (21) of the elite initially trained as schoolteachers, as training was available and free. Only 5 per cent (3) stayed in school education. It was also found in other developing communities that free teacher-training provides the lower classes with opportunities for upward mobility.[1]

The different routes the elite took to advance to the top of their

Table 3.3   First occupation

First occupation	Men % (N)	Women % (N)	Total % (N)
Professional post	62.0 (31)	70.0 (7)	63.3 (38)
Office/shop/laboratory assistant	20.0 (10)	10.0 (1)	18.3 (11)
Factory worker/labourer	16.0 (8)	20.0 (2)	16.7 (10)
Domestic servant	2.0 (1)	–	1.7 (1)
Total	100.0 (50)	100.0 (10)	100.0 (60)

Table 3.4   Reason for entry into first occupation and those still in their first occupation

Reason	% (N)	Still in 1st occupation % (N)
Job was available	36.7 (22)	22.7 (5)
Training was available	21.7 (13)	15.4 (2)
Occupation was 1st choice	26.7 (16)	87.5 (14)
Religious calling	10.0 (6)	100.0 (6)
Family influence	3.3 (2)	100.0 (2)
To get to the city	1.7 (1)	–
Total	100.0 (60)	48.3 (29)

respective occupational hierachies are analysed in Table 3.5. The largest single group were those that stayed in one profession. Half as many again changed professions, while a few more studied for a profession after starting to work.

The role of professional, especially university, training is important to elite recruitment in all societies and has been noted of Africa, Latin America, Western societies, the Middle East as well as Russia.[2]

If one considers that some of the elite included in this study were selected on the basis of their role in community activities and not because of their occupational status, it is noticeable that most of these also had professional training and held senior positions in their occupations.

More than half of the elite had been in their current positions for more than five years, as is evident from Table 3.6. The average time they had spent in this position was 7.8 years (median 6 years),

Table 3.5   Career route taken by the elite

Career progress	Men % (N)	Women % (N)	Total % (N)
Advanced in one profession	50.0 (25)	40.0 (4)	48.3 (29)
Changed professions	22.0 (11)	30.0 (3)	23.3 (14)
Became independent	10.0 (5)	10.0 (1)	10.0 (6)
Studied while a labourer	8.0 (4)	–	6.7 (4)
Hobby became a job	8.0 (4)	–	6.7 (4)
Series of better jobs	2.0 (1)	20.0 (2)	5.0 (3)
Total	100.0 (50)	100.0 (10)	100.0 (60)

Table 3.6   Time the elite have spent in their current position

Time	Men % (N)	Women % (N)	Total % (N)
Up to 2 years	20.0 (10)	20.0 (2)	20.0 (12)
3 to 5 years	26.0 (13)	20.0 (2)	25.0 (15)
6 to 10 years	34.0 (17)	40.0 (4)	35.0 (21)
11 years and longer	20.0 (10)	20.0 (2)	20.0 (12)
Total	100.0 (50)	100.0 (10)	100.0 (60)

demonstrating that they had proved themselves effective and able to meet the demands of their position.

As each career has unique features, eight career histories from different sectors are presented below. All the names are fictitious. In some instances details have been omitted to prevent the identification of personalities although nothing has been added or changed.

The greatest upward mobility within the shortest time occurred in the business sector, probably because opportunities for Africans to advance in the business sector opened relatively late. In the trade unions, people who had been shop stewards or chairmen of work or liaison committees left their jobs to set up trade unions when trade unions for Blacks were legalized in the late 1970s. Others that had been leaders of small unofficial unions prior to legalization, registered and expanded their activities. All the trade unionists started their careers on the shop floor. Most of the entrepreneurs started a small business and built it up. All the managers entered big companies after graduating although most of them had worked elsewhere before studying. Mobility in the business sector is exemplified by the histories of a trade unionist, an entrepreneur and a manager.

Isaac Dlomo: Trade Unionist

Dlomo grew up in a homeland town. His father was a labourer and his mother a teacher. He completed his matric at a boarding school and went into a B.A. full-time with a view to teaching. After qualifying he became a clerk instead, because it offered a better salary than teaching. He spent twelve years as a clerk although there were no advancement opportunities for Africans and they were only employed because White clerks were not available. During this time he became a spokesman for African workers in the system of worker's committees. The committees had no bargaining power and could only relay requests to supervisors. After the legalization of Black trade unions he convened a national meeting of worker committees in his industry which in turn elected a committee to investigate the formation of a trade union. For months the committee members spent all their spare time studying trade unionism and eventually drew up a constitution. The constitution was registered with the government and recognition obtained from management. Dlomo was elected president of the new union, but when it was realised that the president changes annually, he resigned his job to become general secretary. He is now working towards a legal qualification in his spare time.

Thomas Majozi: Entrepreneur

Majozi started his working career as a shop assistant in an up-market general department store in a White metropolitan area. He had a matric certificate. From there he became a health worker in the civil service and did in-service training courses in health. Two years later he was promoted to the post of health assistant. After another year he became a laboratory technician in the same department, which included more in-service training. He worked in laboratories for the next fifteen years being transferred from one hospital to another. He saw opportunities as an independent and, as he enjoyed handiwork, he left state employ to start his own wrought-iron business from his home. The quality of his work was very high and he soon found that large White building contractors were calling him in for their fastidious clients. The mainstream of his business was, however, installing burglar-proofing on credit in township homes. Four years later when he found that collecting his credit was too big a burden, he set up his own butchery. That also lasted for four years until the cold fridges aggravated his asthma. Then, eleven years ago, he set up a chain of supermarkets and bottle stores in African areas. During that time he attended numerous management courses to improve his business acumen and won awards as businessman of the year. He is now in his sixties and does not see himself venturing into anything new.

Steve Ncube: Business Manager

Ncube started his working career with a std. 8 certificate he obtained from a government school on the West Rand. His first job was patching sacks for a milling company. After a year he became a factory hand in a light industry while he did his matric by correspondence. When he had that, he became a clerk and set about attaining a B. Com. degree by correspondence through the University of South Africa. He then became an accounts clerk, a sub-accountant, and upon his graduation a full financial accountant with a multinational pharmaceutical company. This was during the mid-1970s when, because of international pressure, the multinationals gave lots of opportunities to Blacks. Just before the 1976 riots he left for the United States to do an M.B.A. in finance. Two years later he was appointed financial analyst for a diesel manufacturer in Indiana. He then moved to New York where he became an executive trainee with a multinational bank. He was sent to Europe to train as an assistant manager. In 1980 he became manager of an international corporate banking division in New York. Two years later he was transferred to the Johannesburg office, from where he changed to another bank where he was appointed senior executive. He is considering returning to the United States because of the physical danger in South Africa and not being able to live where he would like to because of the Group Areas Act.

All the professionals started their working career with a professional qualification. Many who had started off as teachers went into other professions after having attained further qualifications. Teacher-training was the easiest to attain as many mission institutions accepted students with no means of supporting themselves. Most of the employed professionals made steady progress by continual promotion into higher posts. Mobility in this sector is exemplified by the histories of Gabela and Jama.

Simon Gabela: Attorney

Gabela grew up in a rural homeland with poor, illiterate parents. He reached std 6. at a mission school and then did a three-year teacher-training course at a mission institution. He taught in Pretoria for the next four years while completing his matric by private study. When he had that, he spent three years at an ethnic university completing a B.A. He returned to teaching, this time in Soweto and did his B. Educ. by correspondence. A year later he took up a lectureship at his alma mater while doing an M.A. degree. His political activities at the university led to his resignation and he again returned to school teaching. He spent the next five years at schools in his homeland and in a city while he studied for a legal degree through the University of South Africa. He did his articles and set up practice as an attorney. He went into teaching initially as it was the only profession available to him at the time. He went into law later, as he was able to get sufficient qualifications while he worked to become independent. If he had had a free choice he would have done medicine.

Patrick Jama: Medical Practitioner

Jama was an illegitimate child whose uncle helped him through school. He passed std. 10 at Kilnerton in Pretoria and looked for a bursary to do law. The only financial support he could get was to study medicine, which he did at a city university. He did his internship and planned to specialize. He led a strike of doctors about discrimination against African doctors, comparing conditions at his hospital with others where there was no discrimination. He was forced to resign, and he went into general practice from where he played an active role in organized medicine in the African community. He plans to leave medicine and enter national politics as soon as meaningful opportunities exist for Africans.

The religious sector played an important role in the development of leadership in the African community. Church leaders were able to play a stronger role in the community, for the government avoided restrictions on religious leaders similar to those imposed on leaders in other spheres, as this would have been construed as action against the church. The role that religious elites can play in social change is demonstrated by the experience of Latin America where, after urbanization, the religious elites provided legitimation for moderni- zation and new levels of social integration.[3] Many religious leaders started their careers as school-teachers while they studied for the ministry in their spare time. Others started in the church and ac- cepted more and more responsibilities in church structures. Matipa and Mzamane provide examples of mobility in the religious sector.

David Matipa: Churchman

Matipa grew up in a rural homeland and attended community and mission schools there until he came to Pretoria to do his matric at Kilnerton. He then did a teacher-training course while doing a B.A. and a university education diploma by correspondence through the University of South Africa. Both his parents were qualified teachers. He taught for nine years at schools in his homeland and in Pretoria. He was convicted in terms of security legislation for furthering the aims of an unlawful organization. A charge against him of sabotage failed when he led evidence that he dissuaded youths from setting fire to a Dutch Reformed Church in Pretoria. He spent three years and eight months, of which six months were in solitary confinement, on Robben Island. There he started his theological studies by correspon- dence through Unisa. On his release from jail he was given a clerical post in the offices of the Bantu Administration Department in his homeland, to which he was banished. He complained that he wanted to return to his wife in Pretoria where they had a house. The authorities then promised him a teaching post. One week before he was due to start teaching, he received a banning order, his urban rights were repealed and he and his wife lost their house. He was again restricted to his homeland and was employed in the Depart- ment of Bantu Administration. There he was put in charge of the strongroom where, ironically, all the ammunition was kept. He spent the next two years completing his theological training by correspon- dence. His banning order was relaxed and he became a lecturer at a theological seminary in another part of the country, lecturing on church history and African studies. He then attained an M.A. at the University of Bristol in England. On his return to South Africa he continued to lecture while he filled posts in the structure of his church, until he was appointed to the post of full-time chief executive officer of one of the largest multiracial churches.

Seymore Mzamane: Churchman

Mzamane attended a mission school in a rural area. His father was a migrant worker who did clerical work in a city. His mother was a good gardener and sold the vegetables she produced. After he passed his matric, Mzamane did two years of teacher-training and taught at schools for six years. Then he did two years of theological training and ministered for two years on probation. He spent three years at the University of Fort Hare doing a B.A. in theology. He again did a year's probation in the ministry until he was ordained in a parish. He was there for two years when he left for the United States to do an M.A. in theology. He returned and spent three years tutoring evangelists while he was a mission minister and warden for boarders at a high school. He took up a lecturing post at a seminary and some months later was offered scholarships to Oxford and Harvard universities. He took the Harvard scholarship as it also included residence for his family. He spent five years at Harvard doing his doctorate. When he returned to South Africa he was invited to a lecturing post at a city university, which he declined. He returned to the seminary to lecture while he filled senior organizational posts – including the national leadership – of his church. He became president of his seminary seven years after attaining his doctorate while he was also chief executive of his church, one of the large multiracial churches.

The artists that support themselves started off in low-paying jobs while their art was a leisure activity. When recognition came, they devoted all their time to their art although it was never very lucrative. Others became academics and their art remained a part-time activity. The feminists became involved in their communities and assumed leadership roles among women. The sports administrators (not represented here by a life history) advanced in their field because of their involvement in sport. Many were themselves achievers in sport and their love of the game kept them involved after their retirement from active participation, some in a full-time capacity and others while they practised another occupation. Sithole and Mdlaka provide examples.

George Sithole: Writer

Sithole came to the city from a rural area in his homeland in the early 1960s. He had completed std. 7 at a community school there. His father could not support his family, and his mother did sewing to bring in money, which meant that she did not have time for her children. He was brought up by an aunt who inspired him with tales of his tribal history in which his grandfather had played a prominent role.

He took up employment as a domestic servant in a White household in a city, where he met a tribal healer who tried to persuade his clients to return to tribal customs and traditions. In the urban environment people were very interested in what the healer had to say and they regarded him as a prophet. As a new arrival to the city, the young Sithole soon found himself explaining traditional customs to the people who had been influenced by the healer. He saw a need to write down the meaning of customs so that more people could have access to them.

Two years later he moved to another part of the city, and found domestic employment with the family of a well-known and wealthy White industrialist that came to regard him as part of the family. He started reading the books that were passed around in the house and acquired a love of reading. The family encouraged him to read more and he borrowed books on art and particularly history. It aggrieved him that so little was known about his tribe's art and history, so he set about writing a book on the subject in his spare time. At about the same time he started writing a book with an urbanization theme which he submitted to a SABC literary competition. It arrived long after the closing date but the convenors were sufficiently impressed to recommend that he take it to a university to be appraised. The university staff pointed out that he could not be a successful writer without formal training and recommended that he at least aspire to a university degree. He then set about attaining std. 8 and then std. 10 by correspondence. He enrolled as a first-year student at the University of South Africa while still in domestic employment, but had problems with his employers when he asked for time off to attend vacation schools in Pretoria. They did not believe this reason for his wanting leave. While he was away, his employer's wife broke into his room and found his newly attained matric certificate and Unisa study guides as well as his typewriter and uncompleted manuscripts. She had the certificate framed, and brought in a bookshelf. Neither she nor her daughter, a well-known socialite, had finished school.

Sithole was by now asking for more and more time off to visit libraries to research his assignments and books. His employer set about finding him more challenging employment near the Johannesburg public library, although he would have preferred to remain a domestic servant. Nothing suitable was found in the companies of which his employer was a director, and through an associate he was found a position in banking, which he hated. His employer then arranged employment for him with a firm of White attorneys. He was allowed to retain his room at the industrialist's home.

Sithole started work in the photocopying department, but the other workers saw him as a threat and cast him out. Another employee that had recently arrived from Malawi and was employed as a messenger, pitied his boredom, and invited him to accompany him on his rounds. The writer hated his job and his feet ached, but he nevertheless told the industrialist that he was happy and doing well because he did not want to disappoint his kindness. Later the attorneys appointed him to opening mail, which caused friction with a White woman receptionist who had enjoyed doing the mail. In that position he began to learn about the different branches of the law, as he had to channel mail to the respective partners. On one occasion he put a notice of bar letter, which should have received immediate attention, into the general file, where it lay for weeks. It caused a furore when it was discovered, and the partners pushed him into formal legal training. They pointed out that the B.A. he was doing was useless to him because of the subjects he had chosen. (He had only wanted a degree to make himself acceptable as a writer, and subjects did not matter.) He then enrolled for B. Proc., which was the easiest legal qualification. Again the attorneys pointed out its limitations, as it was not accepted overseas. He then filled his B. A. course with legal subjects and went on to complete his Ll. B. as well as his articles. He was, however, not interested in practising law. By this time he had written books that were prescribed for schools, and he took up an invitation to lecture at a city university where he has subsequently gained an M.A. degree. He would have preferred to stay a domestic servant where he was part of a small family and had lots of time to write. He complains that his university post crowds his life with administrative duties, meeting the ceaseless demands of strangers.

Stella Mdlaka: Feminist

Ms Mdlaka grew up in a well-to-do family educated for many generations. Her father was a businessman and a civic leader in an urban township and her divorced mother the owner of a large farm she inherited before land owned by Africans in 'White' areas was confiscated. Ms Mdlaka left mission school after std. 8 and did a teacher's diploma at a mission institution. She taught happily at schools in Johannesburg and the Orange Free State. She married twice – to a headmaster and, after her divorce, to a businessman. In 1948 when the National Party came to power, she became disillusioned with what they envisaged for African education and looked for new avenues. She then took a diploma at the Jan Hofmeyr School of Social Work. From there she branched into a wide variety of community organizations, devoting herself to the upliftment of the African community in urban as well as rural areas, while she attained further qualifications in social work at the University of the Witwatersrand. During the 1976 riots she spent months in detention without a formal charge being brought against her. She has taken on the national leadership of more than one Black organization, not only for women, and is a world-renowned spokeswoman on conditions in the African community.

The unusually rapid, in some cases spectacular, upward occupational mobility of the elite and the role that higher education played in it, echoes the experience of elites in other developing countries, for example, the Middle East:

> In socio-economic terms, the new elites are clearly 'modern' rather than 'traditional', in the sense of being more educated, more dependent on salaried income, and more secular than their predecessors, often only a generation away from very different social backgrounds from which they have been raised through education. If independence after World War I and II created the revolution in political structures, education has created the sudden changes and opportunities in social promotion, permitting new roles, creating new classes, providing the basis for new struggles for succession and policy direction.[4]

It was also noted of India that education permitted members of lower castes into high-status positions.[5]

Table 3.7   Sector and control of elite employment compared to the RSA
1980 African and White population

	Elite					RSA 1980*	
	Control				*Total*		
Sector	*African*		*White*				*Africans*	*Whites*
	%	(N)	%	(N)	%	(N)	%	%
Public	5.6	(2)	41.7	(10)	20.0	(12)	15.49	34.50
Private:							70.00	65.25
Employee	63.9	(23)	58.3	(14)	61.7	(37)		
Employer	16.7	(6)	–		10.0	(6)		
Self-employed	13.9	(5)	–		8.3	(5)		
Sub-total	94.5	(34)	58.3	(14)	80.0	(48)		
Private households							14.52	0.25
Total	100.0	(36)	100.0	(24)	100.0	(60)	100.00	100.00

*Economically active population.
Source: RSA Population Census 1980, Report 02–80–11

WORKING ENVIRONMENT

Most of the elite were employed in private organizations which were
controlled by Africans, as is shown by Table 3.7. The proportion of
the elite working in private organizations is higher than the general
African population but less than the White population. The large
number of the elite that are employed in organizations controlled by
Africans (which are still rare in South Africa), namely more than a
third, may indicate a preference not to work in an environment
where they have to report to Whites, which has been noticed of
ambitious Africans in general. There is also evidence in this that the
elite might expect the racial discrimination in general society to apply
to a working environment controlled by Whites and undermine their
chances of upward mobility. The desire of upwardly mobile Africans
to be free of White tutelage, assistance, kindness and benevolence
besides domination, was noted by Brandel-Syrier.[6] She records that
successful Africans want to regain their masculinity, self-respect and
dignity. 'A little business of my own', which means freedom from a
White employer, seemed to sum up what the majority of her sample

planned for the future. Reference is made in the next chapter to the elite's wish that their children train for independent careers so that they would not have to work under Whites.

Most of the elite worked in the highly industrialized area of the Witwatersrand where most advanced occupational opportunities are found. This is similar to the pattern for White South African elites as well as for Africa in general, Latin America and the United States, as the head offices of important organizations are usually located in the densely populated metropolitan areas.[7] More than half of the elite (namely 33) worked in Johannesburg and Soweto and seventeen in the other industrialized areas of Pretoria (5), the East Rand (4), Bloemfontein (3), Durban (3), Pietermaritzburg (1) and Port Elizabeth (1). Three worked in towns in the Western Transvaal, Northern Cape and Northern Natal. The other seven worked in homelands, not necessarily the one suggested by their ethnic extraction.

An attempt was made to analyse the status of the elite from the point of view of the number of people to whom they provide leadership. This was not very successful, as the structures in the various sectors are not comparable. It did, however, seem that more than half of the elite, namely 51.7 per cent (31), were responsible for less than ten people, while 13.3 per cent (8) were responsible for more than one hundred people. A total of 18.3 per cent (11) had a White female personal secretary.

INCOME

The annual income of the elite, analysed by sector, is presented in Table 3.8. Their incomes were categorized, and then medians, 25th and 75th percentiles calculated.

It is difficult to interpret their incomes, as every occupation is

Table 3.8   Annual income of the elite by sector (in Rands)

Sector	25th percentile	Median	75th percentile
Business	18 748	28 331	44 165
Religion	4 688	9 375	14 063
Professions	26 880	36 248	50 624
Community life	8 036	17 499	26 498

Table 3.9   Annual income of the elite analysed by level of education

Education	Annual income* (%)										
	1	2	3	4	5	6	7	8	9	10	T
Std. 6	–	–	–	–	–	–	33.3	–	–	–	1.7
Std. 8	8.3	–	28.6	–	–	–	–	–	–	–	6.7
Std. 9	8.3	–	–	–	–	–	–	–	–	–	3.3
Std. 10	–	33.3	14.3	–	–	50.0	–	–	–	–	5.0
Diploma	33.3	–	14.3	–	–	50.0	–	–	–	–	16.7
Degree	50.0	66.7	42.9	100	100	–	66.7	100	100	100	66.7
Total	(24)	(3)	(7)	(6)	(6)	(2)	(3)	(3)	(1)	(5)	(60)

* 1 = Up to R14 999; 2 = R15 000–19 999; 3 = R20 000–24 999; 4 = R25 000–29 999; 5 = R30 000–34 999; 6 = R35 000–39 999; 7 = R40 000–44 999; 8 = R45 000–49 999; 9 = R50 000–54 999; 10 = R55 000+.

renumerated differently and statistics of other groups to which they may be compared are scarce. However, the figures in Table 3.8 show that the income of the professionals was highest, followed by that of those in business. By comparison the religious sector had very low incomes. The low incomes of the religious elite probably explains why a significant proportion of the elite with tertiary education (see Table 3.9) fell into the lowest income category (namely, R15 000 and less). On the other hand, it is noteworthy that almost all in the higher income categories have degrees: of the twelve people that earned more than R40 000 per annum only one did not have a university degree. This indicates that material success among the elite is strongly associated with academic qualifications.

The income of the elite, analysed by their level of education, can be compared with the information obtained by Unisa's Bureau of Market Research in a survey of Johannesburg African households presented in Table 3.10. The Africans in Johannesburg are generally regarded as the most affluent in South Africa. From the tables it seems as though even those elites with no post-school qualification earned much more than the Johannesburg African population. This finding suggests that the African elite are, by and large, a relatively affluent category in comparison with the average urban African population. This has also been noted of elites in White South Africa the United States, Australia, Harare, Nigeria, Uganda, West Africa

Table 3.10   Average annual income of 574 Africans in Johannesburg
analysed by level of education

Education	Men		Women		Total	
	R	%	R	%	R	%
None	4574	4.70	2251	2.74	3835	3.83
Up to std. 4	4498	16.30	2851	18.82	3708	17.42
Std. 5–6	5964	31.66	3159	20.39	5011	26.65
Std. 7–8	6896	19.74	4370	31.37	5483	24.91
Std. 9+10	9163	24.45	6614	20.78	8189	22.82
Diploma	16546	0.62	7530	4.70	8818	2.43
Degree	22442	0.94	4788	0.78	15380	0.87
Unknown	7174	1.56	3120	0.39	6498	1.04
All levels	6866	100.00	4422	100.00	5780	100.00

Source: Extracted from Martins, Unisa Bureau of Market Research, Table
A18, 1986.

Tanzania, Brazil, and India.[8] It has been pointed out that involvement in the modern sector brings high rewards even in poor countries, and that people at the top of the occupational scale are often
found to be renumerated as highly as their counterparts in affluent
industrial countries. They command high salaries because they work
for the same firms, the big multinational corporations, or as medical
practitioners, university professors or senior government officials that
can 'brain-drain' to comparable posts in the West or in international
organizations.[9]

It is difficult to compare the incomes of the elite with those of
Whites, as current statistics are not readily available. The general
magnitude of the difference between African and White incomes is
reflected by Table 3.11. These figures pertain to 1980. Since then all
incomes have increased, while there have been efforts, particularly
within the public sector, to equalize the salaries of the different race
groups. For example, occupations such as nursing and teaching are
remunerated equally in the higher echelons, while more and more of
the lower levels are being equalized.

One way of obtaining a better comparison of incomes is to look at
specific private sector occupations occurring among the elite and to
compare them to occupations in the White population for which

Table 3.11   1980 income of the RSA African and White communities

Income in Rands	% Africans	% Whites
Up to 3 999	98.458	33.13
4 000–5 999	1.033	15.87
6 000–7 999	0.252	14.43
8 000–9 999	0.105	10.32
10 000–12 499	0.062	11.05
12 500–17 499	0.042	8.03
17 500–24 999	0.024	4.29
25 000–29 999	0.004	0.90
30 000–39 999	0.006	0.98
40 000–59 999	0.005	0.55
60 000–79 999	0.006	0.19
80 000–99 999	0.002	0.11
100 000+	0.001	0.13
Total economically active known	100.000	100.00
	(N) (5 115 232)	(2 238 366)

Source: RSA Population Census 1980, Report 02–80–11.

Table 3.12   Selected occupations: comparison of incomes of the elite and RSA White males (in Rands)

Occupation	Elite	Male Whites 1984*		
		25th percentile	Median	75th percentile
Medical doctor	55 000+	36 000	45 300	60 000
Advocate	55 000+	31 500	56 250	90 000
Business owner	42 500	25 300	36 600	50 000
Clergyman	–15 000	13 140	17 290	21 600
Attorney	42 500	31 000	48 000	70 000
Managing director	55 000+	35 000	48 000	71 500
Marketing manager	32 500	32 180	37 310	44 300
Editor	37 500	19 940	24 970	36 080

* *Source*: Extracted from Van Pletzen, HSRC, 1984.

income statistics are available. This was done in respect of seven occupations and the result is presented in Table 3.12. As the incomes of the elite were categorized and individual incomes are not known, the middle value of the income category in which the income occurred was used. Where the incomes were less or more than the categories used, this is indicated. When compared with the medians and 25th and 75th percentiles of 1984 White incomes, the incomes of the elite prove to fit comfortably within the income range of their White equivalents. African elites in the professions and higher occupations thus appear to have incomes more or less comparable to those of Whites in similar occupations, although they appear lower than those for White elites.

MOBILITY CONSTRAINTS

While the system of differential education for the various population groups in the country was not designed to facilitate the upward occupational mobility of Africans in the modern sector of South African society, the system of influx control was meant to limit the settlement of Africans in White-controlled areas. In addition a system of so-called security laws was enacted to obviate resistance to White domination in the modern sector. These control mechanisms manifested in the African community as Bantu education (discussed in Chapter 2), influx control and the activities of the security police, and presented serious constraints on the upward occupational mobility of Africans. While Bantu education and influx control only applied to Africans, everyone was subject to the security laws.

Legal rights to be in the White-controlled areas of South Africa, which included the cities (and known as urban rights), were conditionally extended to certain categories of Africans. Since the early 1950s these were mainly people that had lived in a 'White' area since birth, had lived in the same area continuously for fifteen years or who had worked for one employer for ten years, although the precise definition of who qualified for urban rights was changed from time to time. Certain categories of professionally trained people could get temporary exemption from influx control to practise their professions. All these people were sometimes referred to as 'urban insiders', as opposed to the 'outsiders' who did not qualify for urban rights,[10] while the distinction between insiders and outsiders was enforced by a variety of measures colloqially known as the influx control regulations. A total of 17.25 million Africans were arrested in terms of influx control regulations between 1916 and 1981,[11] while 238 900 were arrested during 1984.[12] Influx control in that form was abandoned during 1986, allowing freedom of movement to all citizens of the Republic of South Africa on a non-discriminatory basis. The status of permanent residents of Transkei, Bophuthatswana, Ciskei and Venda who had lost their South African citizenship when these areas became independent but who are migrant workers in or labour commuters to South Africa, is not, however, settled. There are indications that they might eventually be granted South African citizenship alongside that of their own state.[13]

Slightly more than half of the elite (51.7 per cent, or 31) had urban rights by having been born and having lived continuously in an urban area, while another 1.7 per cent (1) had settled in an urban area before the regulations were promulgated. This means that they would have had no problems with urban rights as long as they were prepared to stay in the specific urban area for which their rights applied. Another 16.7 per cent (10) had been exempted on the grounds that they practised one of a group of highly skilled professions. They would also not have experienced any problems as long as they practised that profession and did not, for example, retire. A total of 11.7 per cent (7) of the elite lived outside the areas where the regulations applied, which meant they would also not have had problems as long as they stayed out of the prescribed areas. A number of the elite (6.7 per cent, or 4) had earned urban rights by complying with predetermined conditions, while 3.3 per cent (2) had had legal wrangles with officialdom to obtain such rights. Five people (8.3 per cent) had managed to live in an urban area illegally.

Although because of their professional and urban background it might appear that the majority of the elite escaped the worst effects of influx control, there are indications that it nevertheless limited their choice of lifestyle and presented hurdles to overcome in their drive for achievement. The importance that was attached to urban rights and the efforts people made to acquire them, is illustrated by the history of a young businessman:

Charles Dlamini grew up in his homeland with barely literate parents. He attended a mission school and after passing std. 8 was awarded a prize for writing the best essay in Northern Transvaal. The prize was a year's tuition in writing at organizations in Zambia, Malawi and Rhodesia. He returned home and worked as a clerk at a hospital as well as a court interpreter. His main ambition at this time was to come to Johannesburg, as this was where 'the world of learning and books is'. He eventually came to Johannesburg for the only work he could get – as construction labourer on contract, in other words as a migrant worker. He worked on a building project carrying pipes. He heard that he could obtain exemption from the influx control regulations if he had a matric certificate. He worked hard and passed his matric in the shortest possible time. When he had this, he found he would need a degree to get exemption from influx control. He enrolled at the University of South Africa for a legal degree by correspondence.

In the meantime, he was discharged from the construction company and his reference book was stamped to the effect that he had only 72 hours to be in Johannesburg and must return to his homeland. He went to see senior officials at the West Rand Administration Board and said he lived too far away to just leave. He explained that he had worked as a court interpreter for the Department of Justice and had in fact been a colleague of theirs. By this time he had found employment with a scale company and he was given the right to be in the city for the duration of a year-long contract. When the time came for him to write his university examinations, the scale company told him to choose between working and writing exams, and he was subsequently fired. He went to see the officials at the administration board again, and his city rights were extended without him having to return to his homeland. This enabled him to take up employment with an educational trust where he was employed as a writer. After eighteen months the publications of the trust were banned, and he took up employment with an oil company as a clerk. This was in 1979 and his employers did not know how to register an African white-collar worker. The administration board again extended his registration as a contract worker.

His company transferred him to a big centre near his homeland as a trainee salesman. When the company wanted to transfer him back to Johannesburg, he said he would come on condition that he could get a house, as he had recently married. With the aid of the company he obtained a house under the 99-year leasehold system although he was still technically a migrant worker.

This was when his letter-writing began. He wrote through the administration board to the commissioner of the Department of Co-operation and Development, and through him to the minister, explaining that he was no longer a labourer but a clerk, and requested exemption from influx control. His request was turned down.

As a law graduate he started presenting papers on tax and company law at Johannesburg conferences, which were also attended by White civil servants. He wrote another letter through the commissioner to the minister pointing this out and asking for exemption from influx control. His request was turned down on the grounds that he was a contract worker and citizen of a homeland.

He continued to follow the prescribed channels and wrote back stating that only the minister could, according to law, take a decision on exemptions and that his submissions had not yet been seen by the minister personally.

He received a telephoned invitation to bring a lawyer and have discussions with senior officials in Pretoria. He replied that he would come alone as he was himself legally trained. Four officials and a lawyer were waiting for him. He put his case to them and pointed out that he had just returned from the United States on an exchange system lecturing at universities. It had been a very unpleasant experience, as he was not seen as an African but as an ordinary South African and was jostled as a protagonist of the apartheid system. He explained that he was embittered as a South African and becoming very frustrated. Officials such as those at the meeting were in the front line and ought to start making friends with people like him. He pointed out that the law provided that professional people be recognised as such, and that the minister was advised by officials such as those present and they ought to help him resolve his problem. The officials replied that he was the citizen of a homeland that would object to him being exempted from influx control. He produced a letter that he had obtained previously from the government of the homeland stating that they in fact had no such objections.

He later received a letter from a deputy minister stating that he had been exempted from influx control.

By this time he, now in his early thirties, had been appointed to a senior post in his company and had been elected president of his professional association. In his position as president he led numerous delegations to meetings with cabinet ministers in Cape Town and Pretoria, which he claims resulted in aspects of the race laws being amended.

An urban professional with attachments to Ciskei, and soon to retire mentioned the impediments influx control had placed on his life:

> My passport is due to expire. When I tried to renew it I was told that I will be a Ciskeian instead of a South African national. That is of no use to me because I can go nowhere as a Ciskeian national. I had a real struggle to get a house. There was so much red tape. I made me feel mad. I made it in the end, but even so I was told I must leave when I stop working, which is in a year or two.

Restrictions on the movement of people also affected the functioning of the African community. A churchman referred to the effect of influx control on family life:

> Our biggest problem is migrant labour. The church is not functioning to the African community because it is not ministering to whole families. In the urban areas it ministers to single men – in the rural areas to women and children only. The church can only function in a family structure. God created the family structure and we shouldn't tamper with that. Marriage officers put people together to have them put apart again by government laws. That is why by choice I am not a marriage officer. It breeds an unstable political situation.

When their career advancement meant accepting higher posts in other areas, influx control presented a new set of hurdles. This was described by a professional and a businessman:

> I earned urban rights as a boy by growing up in Soweto. I lost them when I started teaching in Pretoria. When I moved back to Soweto and took up a post in Johannesburg I got temporary exemption on professional grounds with the help of my employer – after 1976 there was a tendency to be more sympathetic. I have earned them again by working for one employer for a long time.

The experience of the businessman also indicates the arbitrary application of influx control:

> I was born with urban qualifications. I kept them in spite of working in Swaziland for six years. When we came back and applied to buy a house in Soweto, my wife went to the administration board and they actually took our urban rights away because they saw we owned two houses in Garankuwa. I had a big job sorting it all out.

Bantu Education and influx control were central pillars in the government's policy, which was intended to maintain White domination in the modern sector and channel African aspirations to the homelands where they were to exercise their civil rights and, consequently, in the case of people of elite calibre, their need to achieve.

The resistance to the political system shown by upwardly mobile Africans who preferred to live and practise their occupations in the modern sector, made them targets of the security system. While some people were targets because they actively opposed the political system, others elicited the same attention by the very fact of their visible upward mobility which made them symbols of a threat to White domination. The security system consists of a complex of laws which has had the effect of curtailing African political activity. Security legislation provides for the banning of gatherings, people and organizations, restrictions on travel, and detention, deportation and public trials. The laws can be interpreted very widely and are enforced by the security police. During 1984, 1129 people were known to have been detained while 450 names were on the 'banned' list; in 1983, passports were refused to 44 people of whom 25 were Africans, while on 15 February 1984, 358 people of whom 336 were Africans were serving prison sentences in terms of security laws.[14]

When the elite described their occupational activities it soon became evident that the security police also played a prominent role in their lives. (This discussion refers to events before the first declaration of a state of emergency on 20 July 1985.) Fifty members of the elite were consequently asked whether they had had negative experiences of the security police. Only 20 per cent (10) said that they had never been conscious of interest by the security police in their activities, while the other 80 per cent (40) had had various experiences ranging from jail sentences to a consciousness of being watched, as is reflected by Table 3.13.

One of the elite actively helped the security police, which he motivated in this way:

> I feel it is an obligation to give them information. My conscience would worry me if I didn't help because I might in a small way stop more violence.

When they spoke of the role of the security police in their lives, many made comments about the inevitability of the interest displayed in their activities:

> No Black in my position can escape it. I've been questioned and interrogated many times. I've said a number of hard things about education and I have been bothered by them because of it . . . [and] I'd feel a little stupid if they weren't interested in me.

Table 3.13   The elite's worst experience of the security system

Experience	Men % (N)	Women % (N)	Total % (N)
N.a: no experience	17.5 (7)	30.0 (3)	20.0 (10)
N.a: helps security police	2.5 (1)	–	2.0 (1)
Homes/offices searched	27.5 (11)	10.0 (1)	24.0 (12)
Interrogation	12.5 (5)	10.0 (1)	12.0 (6)
Conscious of being watched	10.0 (4)	10.0 (1)	10.0 (5)
Passport refused	5.0 (2)	10.0 (1)	6.0 (3)
Jailed after conviction	5.0 (2)	–	4.0 (2)
Detention without trial	12.5 (5)	30.0 (3)	16.0 (8)
Banned	7.5 (3)	–	6.0 (3)
Total	100.0 (40)	100.0 (10)	100.0 (50)*

* Information only available in respect of 50 people.

The interest of the security police in people in leadership roles is illuminated by the following quotations:

They are watching me carefully. When I made application for a fire-arm this year I was taken to the security police and they started telling me that in 1978 they saw my car outside a political meeting. I can't even remember that I was there. So they must have a file on me.

A churchman referred to visits:

I have had two visits to ask all sorts of questions. They were bad questions about other people and about my personal views. I felt they were dismantling my personality. I was deprived of a passport for a while. It is very satanic especially for church people. If it were not for the Christian church and church leaders this country would have been in flames long ago.

A woman said:

They are watching this organization very closely. They are continually asking members about my leadership, how the organization is growing and where we are forming new branches.

The application of security legislation also has implications for the legitimacy of government-controlled organizations in the African community. A professional man told of how he was interrogated for four hours in 1984 after attending a meeting at a government-controlled research organization. The police interrogated him the following day on opinions he had expressed at the meeting. It was his second interrogation experience and he has since refused to co-operate with any government-linked organization of any matter at all.

MOBILITY ORIENTATION

While it would not provide a complete explanation of elite formation, the orientation of the elite to their own success could be expected to give some indication of what Africans perceive to be the forces active in upward mobility. From a content analysis of the explanations they gave for their success, presented in Table 3.14, it seems that personal characteristics such as self-motivation, courage, flexibility, leadership qualities and a passion for challenges were subjectively seen to have played the most important role.

This reflects the motivational factors called the 'need for achievement', referred to in Chapter 2, which emanate from the internalization of Western cultural values. Broadly speaking, this accords with the findings of other research into the constituents of success in a career among urban African and White adults. A total of 59 per cent of Africans and 73 per cent of Whites said that sheer hard work is the most important factor in success. Fifty per cent of Africans and 52 per cent of Whites considered intelligence to be a key ingredient as well, while, as additional factors, 26 per cent of Africans and 36 per cent of Whites mentioned 'courage to stand up for beliefs', 23 per cent Africans and 34 per cent Whites 'creative ability', 15 per cent Africans and 27 per cent Whites 'people skills', 28 per cent Africans and 19 per cent Whites 'knowing the right people', 17 per cent Africans and 18 per cent Whites 'idealism', and 5 per cent Africans and 10 per cent Whites 'aggressiveness'.[15]

Many of the elite said that self-motivation, drive and determination were the only factors responsible for their upward mobility. This is exemplified by the following quotations:

I strove for the top. There was something in me that said that I

Table 3.14   Explanations the elite offered for their achievement

Reason for achievement	Men %	(N)	Women %	(N)	Total %	(N)
Personality factors:						
Self-motivation/drive/determination	21.2	(24)	19.2	(5)	20.9	(29)
Courage and independence	6.2	(7)	19.2	(5)	8.6	(12)
Passion for challenges	7.1	(8)	3.9	(1)	6.5	(9)
Leadership and communication skills	1.8	(2)	7.7	(2)	2.9	(4)
Flexible and tolerant personality	1.8	(2)	3.9	(1)	2.2	(3)
Sub-total	38.1	(43)	53.9	(14)	41.1	(57)
Values:						
Dedication and hard work	20.4	(23)	15.4	(4)	19.4	(27)
Commitment and loyalty	9.7	(11)	11.5	(3)	10.1	(14)
Exploitation of opportunities	1.8	(2)	–		1.4	(2)
Sub-total	31.9	(36)	26.9	(7)	30.9	(43)
Structural factors:						
Superior education	8.0	(9)	7.7	(2)	7.9	(11)
Privileged family background	6.2	(7)	7.7	(2)	6.5	(9)
Push of parents	5.3	(6)	–		4.3	(6)
Push of relatives	1.8	(2)	–		1.4	(2)
Support of colleagues	0.9	(1)	–		0.7	(1)
Sub-total	22.2	(25)	15.4	(4)	20.8	(29)
Other factors:						
Religious calling/inspiration	7.1	(8)	–		5.8	(8)
White mentor	0.9	(1)	3.9	(1)	1.4	(2)
Sub-total	8.0	(9)	3.9	(1)	7.2	(10)
Total	100.0	(113)	100.0	(26)	100.0	(139)*

* More than one factor could be mentioned.

wanted to be recognised internationally. Since my childhood days I wanted to get to the top.

and

I think journalism is one of those professions where you must be a self-starter. I've tried to be a self-starter. I had to break my way in. I just had to keep pushing and being aggressive.

Table 3.15   Remaining ambitions

Plans	Men % (N)	Women % (N)	Total % (N)
N.a: Have reached the top	44.0 (22)	70.0 (7)	48.3 (29)
Improve competence	42.0 (21)	10.0 (1)	36.7 (22)
Enter a related field	6.0 (3)	–	5.0 (3)
Enter a new field	8.0 (4)	20.0 (2)	10.0 (6)
Total	100.0 (50)	100.0 (10)	100.0 (60)

Among the structural factors, a good home environment was often mentioned. For example:

My home environment. My father was a teacher and a minister. It was a Christian environment. Good home values. Domestic solidarity. There was a Christian touch in our home. I had the advantages of studying as a teacher. It gave me certain rights. Now I have certain privileges as a minister that others don't have.

There were, however, a few people who referred to multiple factors. For example:

The key one is my upbringing. I was very fortunate to have good, supportive parents. I was highly inspired by successful people. I had the tenacity to endure the hardships that I had to go through. I lived through a situation of being in the right place at the right time.

Almost half of the elite (48.3 per cent, or 29) considered that they had advanced the furthest that they were likely to in their field of activity, as is reflected by Table 3.15. Those that thought they had reached the top were mainly over fifty years old, male, and in the religious sector, professions and sport. Those that would like to improve their performance were mainly men, the younger elite and the artists.

Those that would like to become more competent in their field are exemplified by the following:

I think I have reached the top. I have no regrets. I would like to improve in my performance and my work. There must be a time when you say thank-you. All my human aspirations have been taken care of and my problem is how to be grateful to God for what he has given me.

Many reflected on what they might have done although they were satisfied with their lives. For example:

I am a pastor. I always want to be that. I won't change. I would perhaps have liked to be a medical doctor as well. I have a yearning and a hankering for it. I've had fulfilment teaching and ministering. I'm healing souls. I'd have liked to heal bodies as well by being a mission doctor.

Others did have further personal plans. A teacher said:

My ideal is a multi-purpose centre to stimulate children and keep them off the streets. Where they can watch TV. Organized games. Sport. They would also be able to do their homework there. I saw examples of this in Germany. If I had to start again I would do social work.

A performing artist still had many personal ambitions in his occupational field:

What I'd love to do is to open a film and theatre school and train young artists. I'd like to find a space to train young people and stage my own productions. In other words my own company. My training has been a good practical one by observation. The university of life trained me better than an academic university would have done. I learned by experience and watching others.

Others said they would like to enter politics in a new South Africa:

I have reached the pinnacle. I have no other ambitions than perhaps to become a politician in a unified South Africa. But definitely not in the present system.

A little less than half of the elite said that they would do exactly the same if they could replan their careers, as is reflected by Table 3.16. They were mainly the men and the professionals. Those that would

Table 3.16   What the elite would do if they could replan their careers

Alternate career	Men % (N)	Women % (N)	Total % (N)
Exactly the same	42.0 (21)	30.0 (3)	40.0 (24)
Better/more education	40.0 (20)	30.0 (3)	38.3 (23)
Enter a different field	14.0 (7)	40.0 (4)	18.3 (11)
Enter a related field	4.0 (2)	–	3.3 (2)
Total	100.0 (50)	100.0 (10)	100.0 (60)

have liked more or better education were also men, people over fifty and those in the business sector.

The importance of education to upward mobility was again emphasised when they spoke of what they might have done. For example:

I'd take the same course but would go for higher degrees sooner. Even up to a doctorate. It gives one a better platform from which to work. People accept you better the better you are educated.

Although it did not have a direct bearing on their careers, there was nevertheless evidence of a consideration to leave South Africa because of the political situation. For example:

If conditions don't change I'll consider leaving the country to take up a post in academia or the church hierarchy in the US or Canada. I give South Africa five years to change.

CONCLUSION

Having achieved a high level of education, the majority of the elite were able to start their working careers in high-level, often professional, occupations. Others took whatever job was available to enable them to obtain qualifications to move into higher-level occupations later. The drive for achievement which resulted in their high academic qualifications also manifested in their careers and they worked hard to get to the top. They preferred not to work under the supervision of Whites, probably because of a perception that the constraints on African mobility that generally applied in the modern sector of society would also operate in White-controlled organizations. The extent of these constraints, which the elite also had to overcome, is demonstrated by their experiences of influx control and the security system. Their drive for achievement, which is a well-known Western middle-class phenomenon, was confirmed by their assessment of their success being the result of their own efforts.

4 Lifestyle

INTRODUCTION

The African population's initial incorporation into the modern Westernized sector of South African society was in the economic sector. The analysis of the elite's socialization and career development in Chapter 2 and 3 shows that they internalized Western educational and achievement values by virtue of their participation in the modern economy, while they overcame constraints to the upward occupational mobility of Africans to acquire leading positions in modern institutional sectors, in some cases in direct competition with Whites. The question that now arises refers to the extent to which their internalization of Western values is limited to their economic activities and whether they have internalized other aspects of the Western value system. In this chapter, various aspects of their lifestyle (family life, religion, role in voluntary organizations and leisure) are analysed. The meaning they attach to their traditional heritage is discussed in Chapter 5.

FAMILY LIFE

Formation of Marriages

All but three of the elite in the present study had been married. One man and one woman were divorced, and unless otherwise specified are considered with the married ones in the discussion to follow, as they had been married for most of their adulthood and had children. A number of others had been widowed, but had remarried. The marriage form of the elite is reflected by Table 4.1, from which it is evident that most of them were married by Christian ceremony as well as the custom of lobola. (The meaning of lobola is discussed in the next chapter.)

Marriages formed by a Christian ceremony with or without lobola suggests an adherence to the custom current in the African community. Marriages formed by civil ceremony only would suggest a break with conventionality and an indication of secularization. The evidence in Table 4.1 suggests conventionality in the lifestyle of the

Table 4.1   Marriage form of the elite

Marriage form	Men %	Men (N)	Women %	Women (N)	Total %	Total (N)
N.a: Never married	4.0	(2)	10.0	(1)	5.0	(3)
Christian ceremony only	12.0	(6)	20.0	(2)	13.3	(8)
Lobola and Christian ceremony	84.0	(42)	40.0	(4)	76.7	(46)
Civil ceremony only	–		30.0	(3)	5.0	(3)
Total	100.0	(50)	100.0	(10)	100.0	(60)

Table 4.2   How the elite met their spouses

Meeting	%	(N)	%	(N)	%	(N)
Work activities	13.5	(5)	25.0	(2)	15.6	(7)
Family activities	2.7	(1)	–		2.2	(1)
Own social activities	27.0	(10)	25.0	(2)	26.7	(12)
Social activities from parents home	21.6	(8)	12.5	(1)	20.0	(9)
Student activities	18.9	(7)	25.0	(2)	20.0	(9)
Church activities	16.2	(6)	12.5	(1)	15.6	(7)
Total	100.0	(37)	100.0	(8)	100.0	(45)*

* Information not available in respect of fifteen people.

elite. A difference is, however, noticeable in the case of women, of whom almost a third had been married by civil ceremony only. This suggests a higher level of emancipation from tradition among the female elite than among the males.

Most of the elite met their spouses through the usual range of activities, as is reflected by Table 4.2. The evidence suggests that their career environment may have been more important for the selection of spouses for the women than for the men.

When one looks at the educational level of the elite and their spouses as reflected in Table 4.3, it is evident that the spouses had a lower level of education than the elite themselves. In all, 71.9 per cent (41) of the elite had higher qualifications than their spouses, 10.5 per cent (6) had lower qualifications, while 17.5 per cent (10) were at the same level. None of the elite with a school certificate was married

Table 4.3   Educational level of the elite by that of their spouses

Elite's education	Spouses' education							
	1 %	2 %	3 %	4 %	5 %	6 %	Total %	N
Men								
1. Up to std. 9	30.0	15.4	–	–	–	–	12.5	(5)
2. Std.8+9+diploma	20.0	–	11.1	9.1	–	–	7.1	(4)
3. Std 10	–	7.7	22.2	–	–	–	5.4	(3)
4. Std.10+diploma	20.0	23.1	–	–	–	–	10.7	(5)
5. Degree	–	15.4	22.2	18.2	–	–	12.5	(6)
6. Post-graduate	30.0	38.5	44.4	72.7	100.0	100.0	51.8	(25)
Total %	100.0	100.0	100.0	100.0	100.0	100.0	100.0	(48)
(N)	(10)	(13)	(9)	(11)	(2)	(3)		
Women								
1. Up to std. 9	100.0	–	25.0	–	–	–	22.2	(2)
2. Std.8+9+diploma	–	–	–	–	–	–	–	
3. Std 10	–	–	–	–	–	–	–	
4. Std.10+diploma	–	–	–	–	33.3	–	11.1	(1)
5. Degree	–	–	25.0	–	–	–	11.1	(1)
6. Post-graduate	–	–	50.0	–	66.7	100.0	55.5	(5)
Total %	100.0	–	100.0	–	100.0	100.0	100.0	(9)
(N)	(1)		(4)		(3)	(1)		
Total elite								
1. Up to std. 9	36.4	15.4	7.7	–	–	–	12.3	(7)
2. Std.8+9+diploma	18.2	–	7.7	9.1	–	–	7.0	(4)
3. Std 10	–	7.7	15.4	–	–	–	5.3	(3)
4. Std.10+diploma	18.2	23.1	–	–	20.0	–	10.5	(6)
5. Degree	–	15.4	23.1	18.2	–	–	12.3	(7)
6. Post-graduate	27.3	38.5	46.2	72.7	80.0	100.0	52.6	(30)
Total %	100.0	100.0	100.0	100.0	100.0	100.0	100.0	(57)*
(N)	(11)	(13)	(13)	(11)	(5)	(4)		

* Three never married.

Table 4.4   Occupation of the spouses of the elite

Wives	%	(N)	Husbands	%	(N)
Housewife	29.2	(14)	Senior administrator	44.4	(4)
Teacher	22.9	(11)	Own business/indep-	33.3	(3)
Nurse	18.8	(9)	endent professional		
Senior administrator	12.5	(6)	Teacher	22.2	(2)
Own business/indep-	6.3	(3)			
endent professional					
Student	4.2	(2)			
Social worker	2.1	(1)			
Clerk	2.1	(1)			
Factory labourer	2.1	(1)			
Total	100.0	(48)*		100.0	(9)*

* Two men and one woman never married.

to a university graduate, while 51.4 per cent (19) of the elite with degrees were married to someone with a school certificate only. However, when their spouse's education is compared with that of the general African population (which was presented in Table 2.8), it is evident that it is much higher than the average for the African community. In other words, the elite selected marriage partners from the higher-educated section of their community. The need of achievers to marry someone from their own educational level was also noted of the Ugandan elite, where many of the males remained single because of a scarcity of educated women.[1] In the African community of South Africa, male graduates and entrepreneurs were found to marry professional women.[2] It was also noted of other industrialized societies that the elite form status-consistent marriages.[3]

The occupations of the spouses of the elite are presented in Table 4.4. Elites – both male and female – were married to spouses who themselves had achieved career success, or were conventional housewives. Thus approximately half of the wives of male elites had professional occupations such as that of teacher, nurse and social worker. The women elites were married to men in senior administrative posts, teachers, independent professionals and businessmen, which are all high-status occupations in the African community. The large proportion of wives (29.2 per cent) who were housewives suggests that the male elite had Western-conventional conceptions of family life. This is particularly so if one considers the relatively high level of education of the spouses.

Decision-Making and Sex Roles

The families of the elite were all conjugal families, and their family life as indicated by household decision-making and the division of labour seems to differ very little from the ideal-type modern Western family, a pattern noticed of urban African families in general.[4] There was no clear male dominance, while social interaction within the family seemed as intimate as in other modern societies. (This discussion of sex roles is limited to the 55 currently married people.)

In the households where the wife was permanently a housewife, household decision-making was shared more often than in the households where the wife worked outside her home, although there was a high degree of egality overall, as is reflected by Table 4.5. This accords with the experience of elites in tropical Africa, where the pattern of relationships between husband and wife in conjugal families tends towards one of shared roles, greater intimacy and equality, and in Tanzania, where only 46.4 per cent of fathers were the sole decision-maker in their families.[5]

When decision-making is analysed against the geographical background of the elite, as is done in Table 4.6, it is evident that none of the men with a rural background allowed their wives to make the big

Table 4.5 Family decision-making

Decision-maker	Wife's occupation					
	Housewife		Employed		Total	
	%	(N)	%	(N)	%	(N)
In male elite homes:						
Husband	14.3	(2)	30.3	(10)	25.5	(12)
Wife	7.1	(1)	9.1	(3)	8.5	(4)
Both	78.6	(11)	60.6	(20)	66.0	(31)
Total	100.0	(14)	100.0	(33)	100.0	(47)*
In female elite homes:						
Husband	–		–		–	
Wife	–		25.0	(2)	25.0	(2)
Both	–		75.0	(6)	75.0	(6)
Total	–		100.0	(8)	100.0	(8)*

* Three men and two women were either divorced or never married.

Table 4.6   Decision-making in elite families by background

Decision-maker	Background							
	Rural		Town		City		Total	
	%	(N)	%	(N)	%	(N)	%	(N)
In male elite homes:								
Husband	35.3	(6)	16.7	(1)	20.8	(5)	25.5	(12)
Wife	–		16.7	(1)	12.5	(3)	8.5	(4)
Both	64.7	(11)	66.7	(4)	66.7	(16)	66.0	(31)
Total	100.0	(17)	100.0	(6)	100.0	(24)	100.0	(47)*
In female elite homes:								
Husband	–	–	–		–		–	
Wife	–		–		25.0	(2)	25.0	(2)
Both	–		–		75.0	(6)	75.0	(6)
Total	–		–		100.0	(8)	100.0	(8)*

* Five were not married.

decisions alone, while in the case of those with an urban background, 13.3 per cent (4) acknowledged that their wives were the sole decision-makers. In none of the homes of the female elite was the man the sole decision-maker.

This follows the trend in other societies where equality between the sexes is more common in urban environments. It has also been found among the Tswana of South Africa that in urbanized families the husband–wife relationship seems to be assuming a 'partner-equal' pattern in decision-making in almost every sphere of family life.[6] African husbands and wives in Pretoria were found to share decisions on the use of family income.[7] A rural background might indicate a greater adherence to custom, as there was a rigid division of labour with women subordinate to men in traditional African society, and might explain why none of the men from a rural background had a wife who dominated household decision-making.

One of the men explained decision-making from a traditional perspective:

Traditionally there was consultation. There was a religious dimension in that it had to be reported to the ancestors – everyone is involved. The more you are involved in the reality of the decision the more you are involved in the making of the decision. If, for example, the decision involves money and only the man earns, it is only a matter of information and his wife doesn't take part in the decision.

It was sometimes the wife's choice not to get involved with decision-making; for example:

She is steeped in traditional thought. I find it difficult to make her realise she must take certain decisions. The whole domestic scene is in her hands. I don't know what she earns. She saves and she easily helps when I need it. She put in quite a lot when we built a house. She feels that as long as I live she is OK. She leaves it all to me.

Those who believed that the husband should dominate decision-making argued as follows:

It is her responsibility to see to all domestic matters. I'm the policy-maker. I've been given that power by God. At the end of the day one must take the decisions – I do.

More men (male members of the elite as well as the husbands of women members of the elite) helped with the household chores at home (namely 60 per cent, or 33) than did not, as is evident from Table 4.7. Slightly more men helped at home when their wives were employed than when their wives were full-time housewives, although fewer men helped their wives when there were no servants employed in the household than when there were servants. Ironically, the men that helped most with household chores were those whose wives were solely housewives and employed servants (namely 83.4 per cent, or 5), while those that helped the least were the husbands of full-time housewives without servants. This reflects the difference between the traditional division of labour where all household chores are left to the wife, and the influence of modern Western society where men are more amenable to helping with household chores, and is an advance on the rest of the African community where there is not yet a significant difference between the roles of rural and urban spouses.[8]

The specific division of labour within elite households takes many forms. In Table 4.8, household roles are analysed by decision-maker. Although based on small numbers it does seem that where the wife is

Table 4.7 Husband's contribution to household chores

Husband's contribution	Wife's activity									
	Housewife				Employed				Total	
	Servant		No Help		Servant		No Help			
	%	(N)	%	(N)	%	(N)	%	(N)	%	(N)
None	16.7	(1)	62.5	(5)	36.4	(8)	42.1	(8)	40.0	(22)
Heavy/outside work	66.7	(4)	37.5	(3)	31.8	(7)	21.1	(4)	32.7	(18)
Shares all chores	16.7	(1)	—		31.8	(7)	31.6	(6)	25.5	(14)
Most inside chores	—		—		—		5.3	(1)	1.8	(1)
Total	100.0	(6)	100.0	(8)	100.0	(22)	100.0	(19)	100.0	(55)*

* Five were not married.

Table 4.8   Chores analysed by decision-maker

	Decision-maker							
Chores	Husband		Wife		Both		Total	
	%	(N)	%	(N)	%	(N)	%	(N)
Wife runs the house, husband provides	33.3	(4)	–		16.2	(6)	18.2	(10)
Wife works inside, husband outside	33.3	(4)	–		37.8	(14)	32.7	(18)
Children help, husband free	–		33.3	(2)	8.1	(3)	9.1	(5)
Inside chores divided equally	–		16.7	(1)	10.8	(4)	9.1	(5)
Both spouses do all chores	25.0	(3)	–		16.2	(6)	16.4	(9)
Wife does most, husband seldom home	8.3	(1)	16.7	(1)	2.7	(1)	5.5	(3)
Husband lazy	–		33.3	(2)	2.7	(1)	5.5	(3)
Husband does more	–		–		2.7	(1)	1.8	(1)
Both work, servant does all	–		–		2.7	(1)	1.8	(1)
Total	100.0	(12)	100.0	(6)	100.0	(37)	100.0	(55)*

* Five were not married.

the sole decision-maker the husband does less, indicating the wife's dominance and the husband's withdrawal from household matters. In general, however, the figures reflect a traditional division of labour, as in 70.9 per cent (39) of households the wife is involved with inside chores without the help of the husband.

The variety of domestic arrangements is reflected by the following quotations. In a traditional type home, chores were divided as follows:

> I do the housework. He just sits. He sees to the maintenance of the house and electrical things. If he knows I'm at a meeting he would do the housework and the cooking. But only if he feels like it. I won't nag.

Although they don't like doing chores, husbands generally helped when their wives were not available, also indicating that the husbands did not expect their wives to confine themselves to the traditional role of homemaker. For example:

> She does the cooking and domestic chores like cleaning up. Over the weekends I help with the washing up. I care for the kids when she is away on business. I'm father and mother then. She does more domestic chores than I do. I make the big decisions after we discuss it thoroughly. But I'm the boss. Sometimes my wife gets cross about it but that is the way I am.

The conscious effort men sometimes made to accommodate their wife's career was expressed as follows: I try to be liberal. I try not to be difficult. I give her a chance to practise her own skills.

In the minority of homes where the husband helps with inside chores the permutations of chore allocations are endless. The fact that husbands might help with chores such as preparing food and washing clothes was also noticed among the general male population of Soweto, although it is not a general occurrence.[9]

In these three examples of the division of labour in elite homes, the wife works and does not have a domestic servant:

> She tackles the soft things. I tackle the rough things – I even shampoo the floors. We share the kid's homework.

and

> She does the washing and the cleaning while the kids help with the cooking. The kids wash the dishes. I do the ironing as well as some of the cleaning. I do the garden and the repairs. I buy the groceries and the chemist purchases. She gives me a list. I supervise the children's homework.

and

> She does the gardening and cooks. We share the laundry. I do mine and she does hers. The children are taught to do theirs. We have no domestic servant because the children must learn not to be too relaxed. I am mechanically inclined and do the fixing around the house. I like cleaning the cars. I also like cooking but she loves it so I leave it to her mostly.

More than half (55 per cent, or 33) of elite households employed a domestic servant. All the unmarried people employed a servant. Many had complaints about servants; for example:

> Everyone does everything at home. I scrub floors if necessary. We did previously have domestic help but we found our supplies disappearing.

and

> I tend to be dominated by the wife. She does most at home. I do very little because of my hours. I garden occasionally and see to the lights, etc. Domestics are unstable. The agency can only give you those with urban rights. The township girls give more problems than they are worth.

Children

Although their families were not necessarily complete, as 18.3 per cent (11) of the elite were still younger than forty, there was evidence that their families were smaller than those in which they grew up. As is reflected by Table 4.9, the elite grew up in families with an average of 6.5 children (median 6), while they had an average of 3.2 children (median 3). There was an equal number of boys and girls in both families. Their families of procreation are smaller than those of the general African community but slightly larger than those of the White community. In South Africa the fertility rate for Africans was 5.2 in 1980 compared with 2.03 for Whites.[10] The elites therefore tend towards the small family pattern typical of advanced modern societies.

The effect of familial urbanization on the size of families is evident from Table 4.10. Families with less than the median number of children (i.e. 3) were more numerous among the third generation to live in a city, while larger families were more numerous among the first city generation.

Family education did not as yet have such a clear effect on family size, as is evident from Table 4.11.

The age distribution of the elite – some have small children while others have grandchildren – complicates generalizations about the activities of their children. However, the importance of education which the elite expressed in their own drive for education was

Table 4.9   Size of elite families of orientation and procreation

Number of children	Number of families	
	Family of orientation % (N)	Family of procreation % (N)
0	–	1.8 (1)
1	3.3 (2)	10.5 (6)
2	3.3 (2)	28.1 (16)
3	8.3 (5)	19.3 (11)
4	8.3 (5)	21.1 (12)
5	11.7 (7)	17.5 (10)
6	18.3 (11)	1.8 (1)
7	20.0 (12)	–
8	10.0 (6)	–
9	3.3 (2)	–
10	1.7 (1)	–
11	3.3 (2)	–
12	3.3 (2)	–
13	1.7 (1)	–
14	3.3 (2)	–
Total	100.0 (60)	100.0 (57)*
Average	6.5	3.2
Median	6	3

*Three never married.

repeated in their wishes for their children. A typical reaction was that of the father of a young girl: 'I want the best education the country can give her.'

This is similar to the experience in Uganda, where none of the elite thought of their children's future in any terms other than 'as much education as possible', to prepare them for a professional career of some sort;[11] and in Senegal,[12] where the elite wanted their children to take up intellectual professions. This also seems to be the aspiration of the general African population of South Africa: tribal-orientated migrant workers, the urban working class as well as the urban middle class, reveal remarkably similar aspirations for their children, namely secondary education and professional qualifications.[13]

In recent times this has included private schooling since opportunities to attend private schools have become more readily available to Black children. Of the 53 members of the elite in respect of whom

Table 4.10 Number of children analysed by city generation

Number of children	City generation							
	1st		2nd		3rd			Total
	%	(N)	%	(N)	%	(N)	%	(N)
0	9.1	(2)	3.8	(1)	16.7	(1)	7.4	(4)
0	4.5	(1)	15.4	(4)	–		9.3	(5)
2	22.7	(5)	23.1	(6)	50.0	(3)	25.9	(14)
Below median	36.3	(8)	42.3	(11)	66.7	(4)	42.6	(23)
3	13.6	(3)	30.8	(1)	–		20.4	(11)
4	27.3	(6)	15.4	(4)	16.7	(1)	20.4	(11)
5	18.2	(4)	11.5	(3)	16.7	(1)	14.8	(8)
6	4.5	(1)	–		–		1.9	(1)
Above median	50.0	(11)	26.9	(7)	33.4	(2)	37.1	(20)
Total	100.0	(22)	100.0	(26)	100.0	(6)	100.0	(54)*

*Six did not live in a city.

Table 4.11 Number of children analysed by educated generation

Number of children	Educated generation							
	1st		2nd		3rd			Total
	%	(N)	%	(N)	%	(N)	%	(N)
0	9.4	(3)	6.7	(1)	–		8.0	(4)
1	3.1	(1)	20.0	(3)	–		8.0	(4)
2	34.4	(11)	13.3	(2)	33.3	(1)	28.0	(14)
Below median	46.9	(15)	40.0	(6)	33.3	(1)	44.0	(22)
3	21.9	(7)	6.7	(1)	66.7	(2)	20.0	(10)
4	18.8	(6)	40.0	(6)	–		24.0	(12)
5	9.4	(3)	13.3	(2)	–		10.0	(5)
6	3.1	(1)	–		–		2.0	(1)
Above median	31.3	(10)	53.3	(8)	–	(1)	36.0	(18)
Total	100.0	(32)	100.0	(15)	100.0	(3)	100.0	(50)*

*Ten were not educated beyond school.

information was available, 52.8 per cent (28) had sent their children to government schools and 34 per cent (18) to private schools. A total of 11.3 per cent (6) sent some of their children to government and some to private schools, while 1.9 per cent (1) intended sending their children to private schools when they were ready for school. Superior education was the reason given for the choice of private schooling, although there was also a perception that private schools do not prepare children for the reality of South African society. For example:

> As a matter of principle my children must go to government schools. My view is that they should be exposed to the real situation and not be protected. There is a horrifying cultural conflict in private schools as against the dusty townships.

The high aspirations of the elite for their children was reflected by those (50.9 per cent, or 29) that still had children who were minors. When they discussed the kind of future they would like for their children, 58.6 per cent (17) said the choice of career and lifestyle was the prerogative of the child but that they would encourage and help them as much as they could. The others wanted their children to be trained for a career. Many mentioned independent professions; for example:

> I would like to see them in independent careers. My role is to motivate them as far as possible. I have an open mind about the direction.

The preference for independent careers for themselves as well as their children emerged in many interviews. This was related to a perception that people in independent careers escape working in the employ or under the supervision of Whites, and was referred to in Chapter 3.

An analysis of the career progress of the children of the elite shows a predominant preference for higher professions. Of 51 gainfully employed children, 58.8 per cent (30) were in higher professions.

A total of 33 children were university students. Most of them were enrolled for professional training at South African universities while four were studying at universities overseas. The predominant choice of professional careers among the children of the elite echoes the high status attached to these occupations in the general African community. The pattern that is found in European and American studies, that medical doctors, lawyers, headmasters, school inspectors and university professors are the most highly rated workers, has also been found among Africans in Pretoria and Rhodesia: in Rhodesia, the underlying set of norms and values in terms of which these occupations are rated by African communities, is similar to that of industrialized countries all over the world.[14]

A wealthy father of five children who himself had no training beyond std. 6, referred to his children's studies overseas:

> All of them did A-levels at private schools in England. One did a degree in England. One is doing a Ph.D. in Edinburgh. The other three are doing commercial degrees in the United States.

RELIGION

Africans in South Africa were exposed to Christianity and consequently Christian values long before they were exposed to other Western culture patterns. Christian missionaries had established themselves in remote traditional areas and influenced the African population through their religious, health and educative work. Although Africans did not adopt the whole Western culture system at the time, as it was not functional to their traditional lifestyle, the influence of the missionaries may, nevertheless, account for the ease with which Africans later adopted modern culture patterns when they became assimilated into the modern sector of South African society (The later role of mission schools in the education of Africans and the high regard the elite had for the mission institutions, as well as the role of religious activities and Christian values in the early socialization of the elite, was mentioned in Chapter 2.)

Religious observance is still important to the elite, as is reflected by Table 4.12. Only 16.7 per cent (10) hardly ever or never attended church services. The religious observance of the elite fits the general trend of a conventional Western-type lifestyle and the observation that the need to achieve is nurtured in families in which religion emphasizes individual, as contrasted to ritual, contact with God.[15]

It is obvious that the religious elite would attend church services. Of the elites in the other sectors, those that attended services predominated in every age group, although there were less in the higher age groups that hardly ever or never went to church than in the lower

Table 4.12   Attendance at religious services

Attendance	Men % (N)	Women % (N)	Total % (N)
Regularly	60.0 (30)	80.0 (8)	63.3 (38)
Now and then	20.0 (10)	20.0 (2)	20.0 (12)
Hardly ever	2.0 (1)	–	1.7 (1)
Never	18.0 (9)	–	15.0 (9)
Total	100.0 (50)	100.00(10)	100.0 (60)

age groups – 13 per cent (3) of the elite over forty years old compared with 31.8 per cent (7) younger than forty. All ten women attended services, while 71.5 per cent (25) of the men did. Neither the urban/rural background nor the educational level of the elite seemed to play a role in their religious observance. A growth in church attendance among urbanized Africans has often been demonstrated. In the 1970s, nine out of ten Africans in Johannesburg belonged to a Christian church, compared with five out of ten in 1936. In 1972, 92 per cent of Soweto residents belonged to a Christian church. Educated Africans attend church services as often as the uneducated.[16]

The religious affiliation of the elite (including the religious elite) is presented in Table 4.13. A total of 6.7 per cent (4) said that they did not belong to any church, a situation explained by a man as follows:

I do not subscribe to any church. I am not cynical. I am a religious man – I just don't need formal structures.

As is evident from the table, the elite were mainly affiliated to formally organized churches. This accords with information from tropical Africa that the Western educated elite are almost invariably Christian, and is similar to findings from Nigeria that they regularly attend services as members of one of the established churches.[17] The general urban African population of South Africa has also been found to be affiliated to formal churches.[18] An apparent incongruity between the high level of formal Christian commitment and the concomitant practice of traditional religious customs noticed among the elite, is discussed in the next chapter.

Table 4.13   Religious affiliation of the elite

Denomination	Men		Women		Total		African 1980*
	%	(N)	%	(N)	%	(N)	%
Methodist	24.0	(12)	20.0	(2)	23.3	(14)	9.7
Anglican	16.0	(8)	30.0	(3)	18.3	(11)	4.5
Roman Catholic	8.0	(4)	40.0	(4)	13.3	(8)	10.1
Lutheran	16.0	(8)	10.0	(1)	15.0	(9)	4.3
Presbyterian	10.0	(5)	–		8.3	(5)	22.9
Dutch Reformed	6.0	(3)	–		5.0	(3)	0.7
Congregationalist	2.0	(1)	–		1.7	(1)	1.6
Baptist	2.0	(1)	–		1.7	(1)	0.9
Seventh Day Adventist	2.0	(1)	–		1.7	(1)	0.3
Salvation Army	2.0	(1)	–		1.7	(1)	0.2
Christian Science	2.0	(1)	–		1.7	(1)	?
Apostolic Faith Mission	2.0	(1)	–		1.7	(1)	0.6
None	8.0	(4)	–		6.7	(4)	
Total	100.0	(50)	100.0	(10)	100.0	(60)	

Source: RSA, Population Census 1980, Report 02-80-12.

ROLE IN VOLUNTARY ORGANIZATIONS

The prevalence of informal institutions is a characteristic of moder society. People of elite calibre that join informal organizations do no do so to benefit from the activities of these organizations or to fin recreation from tedious work, but because they feel a social re sponsibility to their community. These responsibilities range from personal assistance to assuming organizational office. That the elit were very active in voluntary organizations is reflected by Table 4.14 while 71.7 per cent (43) of them played a leading role in one or mor of the organizations they were affiliated to. It was also noticed i tropical Africa that the elite joined a plethora of voluntary associa tions of Western origin which developed in all the modern towns, an in Nigeria that they played a prominent leadership role in them.[19]

More of the African elite with an urban background (that is 75 pe cent, or 30) played a leadership role in organizations than did thos with a rural background (65 per cent, or 13). Their role in informa institutions is much higher than that of the general African and Whit

Table 4.14   Membership of voluntary organizations

Membership	Male % (N)	Female % (N)	Total % (N)
None	4.0 (2)	–	3.3 (2)
Member of one organization	20.0 (10)	10.0 (1)	18.3 (11)
Member of two organizations	10.0 (5)	–	8.3 (5)
Member of three organizations	66.0 (33)	90.0 (9)	70.0 (42)
Total	100.0 (50)	100.0 (10)	100.0 (60)
Leadership role	68% (34)	90% (9)	71.7% (43)

Table 4.15   Voluntary affiliations of RSA Africans and Whites

Affiliations	%Africans	%Whites
Churches or religious organizations	32	46
Political parties or groupings	4	13
Charities for welfare of people	9	12
Professional associations	8	10
Educational or arts groups	11	8
Youth work (eg. scouts/youth clubs)	10	6
Conservation/environment/animal welfare	1	4
Trade unions	3	2
Consumer groups	3	1
Human rights organizations	5	–
None of these	49	38

Source: Markinor Social Value Study, 1982.

communities, as represented by research done by Markinor in 1982, and reproduced in Table 4.15.

The wide range of organizations the elite are affiliated to, demonstrates the extent to which they are involved in their community and identify with problems at a lower social level. The activities they are involved in and organizations they belong to include the following: family planning, career guidance, professional advice organizations, self-help, Rotary, government advisory councils, professional occupational organizations, sports bodies, educational organizations, school committees, school feeding schemes, youth organizations, SA Institute of Race Relations, Inkatha, organizations concerned with international affairs, church associations, agricultural organizations, university councils, welfare organizations, elected civic bodies, US–SA Leadership Exchange Programme, Urban Foundation, environment protection organizations and women's organizations. The elite preferred not to mention their affiliation to political organizations disfavoured by the government although there were indications that they are active in these organizations. Their affiliation to voluntary organizations shows that they concern themselves with the whole spectrum of community affairs. The strong evidence of the lead they take in these organizations also indicates that their leadership is accepted, which in turn legitimizes their opinion-leader status in the African community.

LEISURE ACTIVITIES

Modern society provides opportunities for creative leisure as less time is needed for subsistence activities. For elites, however, leisure time is largely taken up by voluntary leadership activities in their community. The extent to which the African elite is involved with community activities was shown in the previous section. Most of them remarked that they had very little leisure time for themselves. From the tabulation of their leisure activities in Table 4.16, it is

Table 4.16   Leisure activities of the elite

Leisure activity	%	(N)
Reading	61.7	(37)
Listening to music	33.3	(20)
Watching sport	18.3	(11)
Friends' company	16.7	(10)
Watching television	10.0	(6)
Films	8.3	(5)
Family's company	8.3	(5)
Household activities	8.3	(5)
Nature	3.3	(2)
Catching up on work	3.3	(2)
Photography	3.3	(2)
Listening to the radio	1.7	(1)
Sleeping	1.7	(1)

Table 4.17   Leisure activities of the RSA African and White
communities

Activity	Africans %	Whites %
Sitting and relaxing	18	8
Being active	51	53
Being alone	10	9
Time with family	33	52
Time with friends	36	19
Being in a lively place	12	4
Reading newspapers	64	57
Watching television	58	97

Source: Markinor Social Value Study, 1982.

evident that they spent what spare time they had in quiet solitary
activities and with family and friends.

When one compares their leisure activities to those of the general
African and White communities as presented in Table 4.17, the
elite's choice of solitary activities is emphasized. That being active
and enjoying the company of other people are favoured leisure
activities among the general urban African population, was confirmed by other research in Soweto.[20] The elite obviously did not
need boisterous leisure to balance an existence of mundane routine,
as is the case with the general African and White population.

Books, Newspapers and Music

A modern urban lifestyle provides opportunities to utilize the products of mass communication, the most common of which are printed
matter and music. All of the elite read books. Most were related to
their professional activities. The kind of books they read is presented
in Table 4.18.

Table 4.18   Books read by the elite

Type of books	% (N)
Professional literature	60.0 (36)
Non-fiction	43.3 (26)
Light fiction/novels	36.7 (22)
Serious fiction	23.3 (14)

Table 4.19   Newspapers read by the elite

Newspaper	%	(N)
All available	13.3	(8)
Foreign	6.7	(4)
African	55.0	(33)
Pro-government White	11.7	(7)
Government critical White	85.0	(51)
Financial	8.3	(5)
None	3.3	(2)

By contrast, only 32 per cent of the general African population read any books at all. The purpose of their reading is self-education (26 per cent), recreation (19 per cent), hobbies (15 per cent) and formal study (12 per cent). The books they read are largely paperbacks (24 per cent) and general non-fiction (17 per cent).[21]

Most of the elite read newspapers daily. Two people had had bad experiences with newspapers and journalists and said they did not read them at all. Three people read all the daily newspapers printed in their city, while four subscribed to overseas newspapers. The newspapers they read are presented in Table 4.19.

In addition to the newspapers that they read regularly, they sometimes buy a pro-government Afrikaans newspaper after a specific event to see how the event is portrayed to Afrikaans readers.

The reading pattern of the elite is more sophisticated than that of the general African and White population. In 1985–6, 13.8 per cent of the African and 36.1 per cent of the White communities read a daily English newspaper, while 14.1 per cent of Africans and 46.9 per cent of Whites read an English weekly. Only 8 per cent of the African population read the *Sowetan*, 9.5 per cent the City Press which are African newspapers, and 3.8 per cent the government-critical *Star*.[2] The elite's consumption of printed matter, especially of that printed in English, follows the pattern noticed of the elite in Uganda.[23]

Classical music was most favoured by the elite. Three people said they enjoyed all kinds of music. Their music tastes are presented in Table 4.20.

When one compares this to the music tastes of the general African population, it seems that the elite's music tastes are very sophisticated. According to research done in 1983 by the SABC Listener Research Department for the compilation of television music prog

Table 4.20   Music favoured by the elite

Type of music	% (N)
All kinds	5.0 (3)
Classical	53.3 (32)
Choral	31.7 (19)
Jazz	25.0 (15)
Traditional African	8.3 (5)
Modern African	6.7 (4)
Religious	5.0 (3)
Soul	3.3 (2)
Opera	3.3 (2)
Pop	3.3 (2)
Reggae	1.7 (1)
Spirituals	1.7 (1)
Country	1.7 (1)

grammes, only 5.2 per cent of the African population listens to classical music, compared with popular music (13.3 per cent), choral music (23.6 per cent), disco and reggae (22.9 per cent), jazz (12.3 per cent), modern African music (8.4 per cent), religious music (25.6 per cent), soul (13.8 per cent) and traditional African music (32 per cent).

Sport

Sport is a field which provides both active and passive recreation and is characteristic of a modern lifestyle. In accord with their preference for quieter leisure activities the elite enjoyed watching sport on television more than they did going to a sports meeting or taking part themselves. Those that did take part gave preference to tennis and golf, which are sports enjoyed by the more affluent people in other industrialized societies. These sports are also easier to fit into the full work schedule of busy people. Their sporting interests and means of expressing them are presented in Table 4.21.

Forty per cent of the elite participated in a sport, and 51.7 per cent attended sports meetings, which is higher than the figures for the general African and White communities. In 1985–6, 9.1 per cent of Africans and 24.2 per cent of Whites took part in sport in the preceding twelve months, while 11.3 per cent of Africans and 26.6 per cent of Whites were spectators at sports meetings in the same

Table 4.21   The elite's interest in sport

Watched on television	% (N)	Spectator at sport meeting	% (N)	Active participator	% (N)
None	20.0 (12)	None	51.7 (31)	None	60.0 (36)
Soccer	60.0 (36)	Soccer	33.3 (20)	Tennis	15.0 (9)
Tennis	35.0 (21)	Boxing	10.0 (6)	Golf	10.0 (6)
Boxing	20.0 (12)	Tennis	3.3 (2)	Jogging	6.7 (4)
Rugby	13.3 (8)	Cricket	3.3 (2)	Exercises	6.7 (4)
Wrestling	5.0 (3)	Athletics	3.3 (2)	Netball	1.7 (1)
Cricket	5.0 (3)	Golf	3.3 (2)	Cycling	1.7 (1)
Athletics	5.0 (3)	Bodybuilding	1.7 (1)	Swimming	1.7 (1)
Golf	3.3 (2)	Softball	1.7 (1)		
Softball	1.7 (1)	Wrestling	1.7 (1)		
Bodybuilding	1.7 (1)	Baseball	1.7 (1)		

period.[24] The sports the people of Soweto participate in most are soccer, athletics, boxing, swimming, body-building and tennis, in that order,[25] confirming a contrast with the elite that preferred sports that were better suited to their busy lifestyle. It was mostly the male members of the elite that participated in sport, which was also found to be the case in the general African population.[26]

HOLIDAYS WITHIN AND TRAVEL OUTSIDE SOUTH AFRICA

A high level of occupational involvement, complex employment practices which include service benefits, as well as high incomes and interests outside their immediate environment, provide people with an impetus to explore other localities, and is reflected by holiday and travel activities. The holiday activities of the elite are presented in Table 4.22.

Table 4.22   Holiday activities of the elite

Holiday activities	% (N)
Do not take holidays	21.7 (13)
Conventional activities	61.7 (37)
Local commercial holidays	38.3 (23)
Overseas commercial holidays	13.3 (8)

Table 4.23   World travel experience of the elite

Area visited	% (N)
None	5.0 (3)
The whole world	3.3 (2)
North America	78.3 (47)
United Kingdom	70.0 (42)
Rest of Europe	65.0 (39)
Former Protectorates	66.7 (40)
Rest of Africa	35.0 (21)
Far East	21.7 (13)
Middle East	18.3 (11)
Australasia	10.0 (6)
Scandinavia	10.0 (6)
Eastern Europe	8.3 (5)
South America	6.7 (4)

Most of them had conventional holidays relaxing at home, visiting relatives and friends, working on their farm or catching up on work. Others took commercial holidays touring South Africa, going to the sea or visiting game reserves, while some took commercial holidays overseas.

All but three had visited countries outside South Africa, while two had travelled around the world and preferred to mention the countries they had not visited. In most cases overseas travel was connected with their work and was by invitation. Many of them went overseas more than once a year. The areas they visited are presented in Table 4.23

When these figures are compared with those of the African and White communities, it is evident that the elite are exceptionally well travelled. Although the figures are not strictly comparable, there is some indication that in 1985–6, 0.1 per cent of Africans had travelled overseas by air on business and 0.02 per cent on holiday during the preceding twelve months. The respective figures for Whites are 2.3 per cent on business and 5.8 per cent on holiday.[27] The wide experience of elites of travel to foreign countries was also noted of other societies. In most cases their experience of other societies was the result of higher education in modern countries. In Nigeria, 88 per cent of the elite had enjoyed significant foreign residence or travel in a Western country, while 37 per cent of the legislative and 55 per cent of the administrative elite of Tanzania had studied in developed countries.[28] This trend was also noted of Brazil, Egypt, Saudi Arabia and Turkey.[29]

These leisure activities, reading and travelling patterns show the elite to be consumers of Western culture products.

LIFESTYLE INCONGRUITIES

The assimilation of the elite into the modern sector of South African society is evident from their career activities as described in Chapter 3 and their lifestyle described in this chapter. An attempt was made to ascertain possible incongruities between their lifestyle and modern society by looking at their perception of existential problems. This was done by means of the question: 'What bugs you most about life?' Problems on the societal level were mentioned more than any other, as is reflected by Table 4.24.

Problems on the societal level were largely related to the socio-political system, and affected the elite individually; for example:

I am not a fulfilled person perhaps due to the society in which I live. I can't live in a decent area with trees. I can't move and live where I want to. I can't make meaningful choices in a nice decent suburb. I like to go to movies. There are nice ones in Sandton but I can't go. I am limited in my choices by apartheid.

The socio-political system also manifested collectively:

The disruption of family life. If the family was a unit as it ought to be we'd have a better-quality citizen and politician – a homely type of person. I know families where the mother lives with the baby for three months. When she starts working she never sees the child.

Table 4.24   Existential problems experienced by the elite

Problems	% (N)
Societal	73.3 (44)
Interpersonal	30.0 (18)
Personal	5.0 (3)
Occupational	3.3 (2)
None	5.0 (3)

The grandmother takes over. The mother leaves home before the child wakes up. The child never gets a chance with its parents. What kind of society are we building? Are you surprised they are rioting? Fathers never see their families. He thinks of his wife as a babymaking machine and of his children as a lifelong burden. We can change all this with socio-economic change. That is the route for change.

The violence in the country was mentioned many times. For example:

I'm concerned about my country. Endemic violence is tearing the soul of this nation apart.

and

The political system in South Africa. Conflict. Our children are absorbing aggression as a way of life.

Interpersonal problems are exemplified by the following:

Human attitudes. People's attitudes. I take them as incapable of living together. Politicians of any colour. I hate them. They totally lack morality. They even use children for their own ends as in the townships now.

CONCLUSION

The lifestyle of the elite as indicated by their family life, role in voluntary organizations and leisure activities shows that they have fully internalized the modern Western value system already dominant in the White community of South Africa. Various writers have pointed out that the value system and lifestyle of the general modernized African population resembles that of Whites,[30] while the same pattern has been noticed of African elites in the rest of Africa.[31] The elite therefore displayed the same internalization of Western values noted of other categories in the process of modernization, while their affluence and access to facilities emanating from their high social status would put them ahead of the rest of the community in their socialization in terms of Western culture patterns.

Their prominent role in voluntary organizations in addition to their occupational leadership suggests that their leadership is accepted by the general African population. This legitimizes their status as opinion-leaders and suggests that they serve as role models to the general African community.

5 Traditionality

INTRODUCTION

The spread of modernity around the world and the intellectual construction of a traditional-modern continuum has, sometimes, erroneously been interpreted as though traditionality and modernity are mutually exclusive and that modern societies are traditionless. The experience of other societies has demonstrated that modernization does not mean that societies undergoing change relinquish their traditions, or that there is no attachment to customs and ways of the past or to symbols of collective identity. On the contrary, modernity has been shown to affect only one specific aspect of traditionality, namely the legitimation of the social, political and cultural orders in terms of traditional symbols, while it has given rise to a continuous process of reconstitution of the other aspects of tradition.[1] This process is relevant to the African elite of South Africa as they are a fully Westernized category of people, while as part of the general African population which is known for its traditional heritage, they have been excluded from the societal community. The traditionality and particularly the ethnic extraction of the African population of South Africa has been interpreted in various ways, among others as a basis for the political ordering of South African society. As was pointed out in Chapter 1, it became official policy after 1948 that the Africans should exercise their civil rights in homelands where a traditional lifestyle predominates, while measures were taken to discourage their upward mobility in the modern sector of society. The traditional lifestyle of many Africans and the supposedly irreconcilable differences between the various African groupings, were used as motivation for the policy. Politically, ethnic differentiation was seen as a way of ensuring that the numerical ratio between Whites and non-Whites was kept manageable and that the White minority would not be confronted by one huge non-White majority, and has been referred to as the 'political strategy of ethnic mobilization'.[2]

In other parts of Africa, economic development and the subsequent spread of education has led to what have also been called the tendencies of 'traditionalism' and 'progress' or modernity. The traditionalist tendency is the perception of the future of society as a transformation of the typically African culture of the past into a new, neo-African culture, retaining the spirit of many institutions such as the family, social and political systems. On the other hand, the progressive school considers the old order of things to be no longer suitable for contemporary life and hopes for a democratic political system, a rational economic system based on industrialization and the rejection of anything which might hinder the society's movement towards Western civilization.[3]

It has also been pointed out that people who are designated traditionalists or modernists are neither exclusively one nor the other. What distinguishes the two is the basic orientation by which a person seeks to gain prestige or esteem. A man who lives according to tribal norms is a traditionalist, though he may work for a modern commercial enterprise, and a man who leads a European way of life is a modernist, even though he will occasionally wear native clothing and interact with his own tribal traditionalists according to their standards.[4] The salience of these tendencies of traditionalism and modernism has been recorded by many writers.[5] The result has been the emergence of modern elites alongside the traditional ones. The consequences of this dichotomy have not been disintegrative for society as a whole, as all the elements of African societies keep in touch with one another through the extended family system,[6] while young people tend to identify with the modern elite.[7] The ubiquitous kinship system has ensured that elites maintain close affective ties with people at a much lower social level, and has been offered as an explanation for the absence of elite cohesion and consequently class consciousness in Africa.[8]

The experience of Africa has shown that modern elites, although cosmopolitan and antiparochial, do not sever their ethnic and kinship links. They are proud of their tribal histories and participate in tribal activities and observe the traditional modes of respect when they interact with their tribesmen. On the other hand, their tribes honour them for their social and professional achievements in the modern world. These ethnic associations have been seen as the most important factor preventing the modern elites in Africa from forming a distinct social class. The modern elites also show no emotional conflicts as a result of shifting between modern and traditional social contexts.[9]

African societies recognise the prestige of the new intellectual elites and their opinions carry as much weight as those of traditional leaders.[10] The modern elites are often the only people capable of healing serious breaches between intra-ethnic factions, while they play an important, active role in community and national integration.[11]

Ethnicity is not a rigid attachment but competes with other associations depending on what is most functional in any situation at a specific time. In other words, ethnicity has to be mobilized to become an independent reality.[12] Ethnicism was given a bad reputation by events such as the Nigerian civil war, Katanga separatism in Zaire and Buganda separatism in Uganda, and it is not surprising that modern African leaders play down tribal differences in the name of nation-building. A nation state with a common language and common citizenship has come to be regarded as the badge of modernity, while ethnicism is associated with backwardness.[13]

In this chapter the identification of the African elite of South Africa with their traditional heritage is analysed. The meaning of their ethnic extraction is analysed, as well as its manifestation in marital selection and language use. The practice of two well-known customs – lobola and ancestor veneration – is analysed as indicators of their participation in traditional customs. These customs have the same content and meaning for all ethnic groups.

ETHNIC IDENTIFICATION

A consequence of the government's policy of ethnic differentiation was the allocation to every African of an ethnic identity. This classification labelled an African as a member of a specific ethnic group and implied that he was affiliated to the corresponding homeland. His ethnic identity also determined other aspects of his life such as where he could live and work and which schools his children attended. After changes to legislation during 1986, Africans other than those ethnically affiliated to the Transkei, Bophuthatswana, Venda and Ciskei were no longer considered to be politically connected to a homeland, which means that ethnicity has in some respects lost its official significance.

Ethnologists distinguish five broad ethnic divisions among Africans in South Africa, namely the Nguni (comprising the Zulu, Xhosa, Swazi and Ndebele groups), Sotho (the Northern and Southern Sotho and the Tswana groups), Shangane/Tsonga, Venda, and a small scattered group, the Lemba.[14] The South African ethnic groups including the people of Zimbabwe, Zambia, Mozambique, Botswana and Namibia are collectively known as the Southern Bantu, and are

Table 5.1   Ethnic extraction of the elite compared to the African
population of Greater South Africa

| Ethnic group | Elite | | | S.A* |
	Men % (N)	Women % (N)	Total % (N)	%
Zulu	30.0 (15)	30.0 (3)	30.0 (18)	27.53
Tswana	22.0 (11)	30.0 (3)	23.3 (14)	11.41
N. Sotho	22.0 (11)	–	18.3 (11)	11.37
S. Sotho	6.0 (3)	20.0 (2)	8.3 (5)	8.44
Xhosa	6.0 (3)	10.0 (1)	6.7 (4)	26.58
Ndebele	4.0 (2)	–	3.3 (2)	3.19
Venda	4.0 (2)	–	3.3 (2)	2.51
Swazi	2.0 (1)	10.0 (1)	3.3 (2)	4.14
Shangaan	4.0 (2)	–	3.3 (2)	4.82†
Total	100.0 (50)	100.0 (10)	100.0 (60)*	

*Includes Transkei, Bophuthatswana, Ciskei and Venda; *Source*: SA
Statistics 1982, combined with unpublished statistics from the Southern
Africa Development Bank.
†Includes Tsongas.

distinguished as a group from the other black groups of Africa on
linguistic criteria, while their mode of life, social organization and
religious system show broad resemblances.[15] The various groups in
South Africa have been allocated politically to the homelands of
Kwazulu (Zulus), Transkei (Xhosas), Ciskei (Xhosas), KaNgwane
(Swazis), Kwandebele (Southern Ndebeles), Lebowa (Northern
Ndebeles and Northern Sothos), Bophuthatswana (Tswanas), Qwa-
Qwa (Southern Sothos), Gazankulu (Shangaans and Tsongas), and
Venda (Vendas). The total geographic area of the homelands com-
prises 13 per cent of the total land area of South Africa while, in
1980, 47 per cent or 10 121 420, of the African population lived
outside the homelands. Another 47 per cent or 10 093 344, live in the
homeland implied by their ethnic extraction, while 6 per cent or 1.2
million, lived in the 'wrong' homeland. The ethnic extraction of the
elite is presented in Table 5.1. Their ethnic extraction more or less
reflects the ethnic divisions in the African population.

The meaning of ethnicity has been approached in various ways.
One important indicator of ethnic group solidarity is the ethnic
composition of marriages, as was pointed out by Drachsler in 1920
and still widely quoted:

Table 5.2   Ethnic composition of elite marriages

Ethnic composition	% (N)
N.a: not married	5.0 (3)
Different ethnic group	43.3 (26)
Same ethnic group	38.3 (23)
Same division but different group	13.3 (8)
Total	100.0 (60)

> Individuals who freely pass in marriage from one ethnic circle to another are not under the spell of an intense cultural or social consciousness. Consequently the greater the number of mixed marriages, the weaker, broadly speaking, the group solidarity.

The ethnic composition of elite marriages was analysed and is presented in Table 5.2.

When one considers that only 38.3 per cent (23) of the elite of this study married someone from the same ethnic group as themselves, and that marriages generally occur between people of similar background and characteristics, it would seem that ethnicity as indicated by marital selection is not important to the elite. It was noticed among the elite in tropical Africa that the smaller the size of the elite the greater the proportion of mixed marriages. As education, especially that of women, expands, the greater the chance that the male elite will find suitable spouses within their own ethnic group. Half of the Yoruba university graduates in Ibadan found wives from the same ethnic sub-group as themselves, for example, while the Zambian elite had a very high proportion of mixed marriages.[16] Because of the underdevelopment of the traditional homelands in South Africa, most of the educated Africans, including the elite, live in the modern industrial areas, where people from all ethnic groups meet and it was to be expected that they would marry people who matched their educational status rather than their ethnic background. Other research has found that ethnicity has very little to do with the choice of friends, and that interests and educational level are more important than ethnicity:[17] in 1965, 29 per cent of Soweto residents married outside their ethnic group.[18] Later research found an even greater tolerance of inter-ethnic marriage: in 1981, 85.5 per cent of the residents of Soweto said that there was nothing wrong with marrying someone from another ethnic group, as did 78.1 per cent from Garankuwa and Mabopane near Pretoria, 66.1 per cent from the ethnically homogenous areas of Madadeni and Osizweni in Kwazulu, and 83.1 per cent in Sibasa, the main town in Venda.[19] It was pointed out in Chapter 4 that 77.8 per cent of the elite met their spouses away from the environment of their parental home, and that they married people with a educational background similar to their own. Even in traditional African society there were no barriers to intermarriage; women adopted the culture patterns of their husband's ethnic group, which were in any case similar to their own.

Whatever the cause of intermarriage, its consequence among Africans, and displayed here by the elite as a leadership group, is the accelerated development of a common identity among the various ethnic groups. This also has a bearing on the language the elite speak at home, as language is universally regarded as the most important culture symbol. However, as the cultures of the various ethnic groups are very similar and their languages are related, the African language or combination of African languages the elite speak at home in relation to their ethnic group is less important than their use of a Western language when their traditionality is considered. The language use of the elite with an indication of its traditionality is presented in Table 5.3.

Table 5.3   Language use in the homes of the elite

Language use	% (N)
Traditional:	
Spouses from same group, speak that language	29.8 (17)
Husband's language	17.5 (10)
Wife's language	3.5 (2)
Unrelated to either's ethnic group	1.8 (1)
Subtotal	52.6 (3)
Non-traditional:	
Township mixture	26.3 (15)
English only	17.5 (10)
Spouses language the same with English	3.5 (2)
Subtotal	47.3 (27)
Total	100.0 (57)*

*The home language of the three unmarried people is unknown.

It is evident from Table 5.3 that a little less than half (namely 47.4 per cent or 27) did not maintain the general traditional pattern of language usage. More than a quarter spoke what they referred to as a 'township mixture'. Children in the Transvaal urban areas grow up in townships that are ethnically mixed, which means that neighbours often speak different languages. From their street games they learn all the languages and then perpetuate the 'township mixture' in their own families, mixing different languages in the same conversation, even in one sentence. The mixture includes English and sometimes Afrikaans, with different languages used for different purposes. This was also noticed in the languages heard in waiting-rooms before interviews took place. In their day-to-day dealings with the affairs of their employers, secretaries and receptionists mixed their languages in one conversation, with English and Afrikaans included if these languages had an appropriate phrase or explained a point more succinctly. This indicates an adaptation to the modern environment where English is the predominant language and a plethora of languages is disfunctional, although a traditional language use is still strongly evident.

The evidence of the vagueness of their traditional heritage is, however, much stronger when the meaning the elite attached to their ethnic extraction is analysed on the basis of a specific question on the issue, as is done in Table 5.4. Almost three-quarters (70 per cent or 42) did not identify with their ethnic extraction, while 30 per cent (18) attached varying importance to it. The low level of identification among the women is also significant, as mothers in modern society generally play a greater role than men in the socialization of children.

Although neither age nor educational level had an effect on the level of their identification with their ethnic extraction, their geographical background did, however, seem to play a role, as is evident from Table 5.5. Those with a rural background displayed a greater identification with their ethnic extraction than did those with an urban background – probably, *inter alia*, because most rural areas are ethnically fairly homogeneous and do not provide opportunities for inter-ethnic contact.

As is shown in Table 5.6, even those that identified with their ethnic extraction had not married someone from their own ethnic group. It might also to some extent have been fortuitous that those that identified with their ethnic extraction married someone from the same ethnic group, as other criteria, such as educational level, play an important role in marital selection.

The greatest rejection of ethnicism came from the professional and

Table 5.4   The meaning the elite attach to their ethnic extraction

Meaning of ethnic extraction	Men % (N)	Women % (N)	Total % (N)
Ethnic identification present:			
Engenders pride but has no implications	8.0 (4)	30.0 (3)	11.7 (7)
Culturally important, otherwise irrelevant	12.0 (6)	–	10.0 (6)
Very important, lives in a homeland	6.0 (3)	–	5.0 (3)
Important, would prefer to live in a homeland	4.0 (2)	–	3.3 (2)
Subtotal	30.0 (15)	30.0 (3)	30.0 (18)
No ethnic identification:			
Nothing	52.0 (26)	40.0 (4)	50.0 (30)
Being Black in South Africa	12.0 (6)	30.0 (3)	15.0 (9)
Relevant only as a language	6.0 (3)	–	5.0 (3)
Subtotal	70.0 (35)	70.0 (7)	70.0 (42)
Total	100.0 (50)	100.0 (10)	100.0 (60)

Table 5.5   Ethnic identification according to background

Ethnic identification	Rural % (N)	Urban % (N)
Present	50.0 (10)	20.0 (8)
None	50.0 (10)	80.0 (32)
Total	100.0 (20)	100.0 (40)

economic elites – 86.6 per cent (13) and 73.3 per cent (11) respectively did not identify with their ethnic extraction. In all the other sectors 60 per cent attached no importance to their ethnic identity.

The low level of ethnicism displayed by the elite is supported by other research done among the general urban African population. In 1980 it was found that only 13.5 per cent of urban men had a certificate of citizenship of a homeland,[20] while in 1983 three-quarters

Table 5.6   Marriage according to ethnic identification

| Spouse | Ethnic identification | | Total |
	Important % (N)	Unimportant % (N)	% (N)
Same ethnic group	43.8 (7)	39.0 (16)	40.4 (23)
Different ethnic group	56.3 (9)	61.0 (25)	59.6 (34)
Total	100.0 (16)	100.0 (41)	100.0 (57)*

*Three never married.

of urban men had limited or no economic, social, religious, emotional or political bonds with a homeland.[21] Research in 1986 among urban women found that only 13 per cent felt they belonged to a homeland; only 29 per cent regarded themselves first and foremost as members of their ethnic group, 38 per cent regarded themselves first and foremost as Blacks, while 33 per cent considered themselves South Africans first.[22] The Buthelezi Commission found that the phenomenon of Zulu ethnicism is essentially limited to the very unskilled, poorly educated people.[23] As the earlier planning of Soweto was done in such a way that members of similar ethnic groups reside in the same suburb, ethnic residential grouping has received much attention in research. In 1965 it was found that the vast majority of people in Soweto did not see anything positive in ethnic grouping, whether they were born in Soweto or not. The dislike of ethnic grouping was just as prevalent among the more as among the less tribally orientated people.[24] In 1972 it was found that urban Africans rejected ethnic groupings, as it was seen to divide the African community.[25] In 1981 a large housing survey revealed that only 11 per cent of Soweto residents supported the idea that residential areas be organized on an ethnic basis, compared with 15 per cent of the residents of Mabopane and Garankuwa near Pretoria, 32.8 per cent of the residents of Madadeni and Osizweni in Kwazulu, and 25.5 per cent of the residents of Sibasa, the main centre of Venda.[26]

The ambiguities inherent in the whole issue of ethnic identification are illustrated by one of the men in the study who practises traditional medicine as a hobby. His grandmother, who brought him up, was a healer, but when he became a Christian in his early teens he rejected it and stayed clear of any involvement. When he came to the city to practise his profession and saw so much disease in those around him, he applied what remedies he could remember from his grandmother. When he found he was successful he returned to his grandmother to learn all he could. He now runs a traditional practice in his spare time, working closely with conventional medical doctors, although he must endure the chagrin of his wife, while he hides all knowledge of it from his professional colleagues. He described the meaning of ethnicity as follows:

> Ethnicity is important. People come to me for medicine. I won't take a second wife for practical and ethical reasons. I feel no affinity for my homeland – we must overcome it because it divides people. I speak Venda to my wife and children. I visit there regularly – I go to the mountains to get herbs. I'd never consider living there. I want to be buried there, though. That is the only connection. You don't get a proper funeral in town. Coffins are stolen and second-hand ones sold.

The elite's, and indeed the broader African community's, strong rejection of ethnicism might be explained by the incorporation of the African population into the industrialized sector of South African society and the concomitant weakening of traditional attachments. At the same time, the similarity of the culture patterns of the different ethnic groups has increased the revulsion Africans feel at the political importance their ethnicity has been given as an instrument attempting to deny Africans participation in the societal community. The elite might feel this more severely than the rest of the African population. It has also been documented in regard to elites in tropical Africa that 'tribalism' is denigrated among the upwardly mobile. Factions based on ethnic groups have been seen as a threat to national independence and aspirations to unity, so that it became a handicap to be too closely identified with an ethnic group and preferable to assume ethnic neutrality.[27]

The elite described the meaning of their ethnic identification in various ways. Those for whom their ethnicity meant nothing compared Africans to other nationalities; for example:

> It means nothing. I could have been anything like Xhosa or Zulu. I do have high esteem for Sotho leaders as individuals but I don't hero-worship them. They can't do anything for me. Just as the Afrikaner can't say he is of German origin and a German, I am not

a Sotho. I don't have any dealings with a homeland. It is stupid to put people into cells. My parents were Sotho but I learnt all the other languages on the street. All the neighbours belonged to different language groups so I learnt them all. At home we speak a mixture of languages. My children speak Zulu mainly.

and

I can't explain more than that it is just the clan that I grew up in. Nothing more than that. We are all Black people together. We are even closer together than the English, Scots, and Irish. To lay accent on it just divides people unnecessarily.

Others regarded their ethnic classification as a product of officialdom. For example:

I don't belong to an ethnic group really. I've been classified as Ndebele. I can't even speak the language. We speak a mixture of mainly English and Sotho at home.

and

My classification as Tswana means nothing. It was given to us when we went to get a pass. We were nothing before then. We don't know their culture. We speak Zulu, Sotho and English at home – sometimes all in one sentence. I'd really have to think and concentrate if I had to speak pure Sotho to someone from Lesotho.

The limitations of ethnic identity were also expressed; for example:

It doesn't mean much. Ethnic matters are limiting. I am interested in mankind and try to indicate this in my behaviour and everything else. Ethnic extraction is incidental – not out of disrespect for my parents or anything like that but I don't think that I have to give it any more credence than it is worth.

The politicization of ethnicity was repulsive to some:

It means nothing to me now because of Inkatha. Inkatha has made me ashamed of being a Zulu. It evokes a militaristic image – an image of tribalistic Shaka. It is an image which I find repulsive. Inkatha has overshadowed the beauty of the Zulu. I wouldn't vote for Buthelezi because I don't like his fanatical Zulu orientation.

For another group of people the meaning of their ethnic extraction lay in their African identity. For example:

It means nothing really. I'm a South African human being. I hate stress being laid on ethnicity. I like my Africanness rather than my Xhosaness because of what it has meant in terms of my personal philosophies and religion. It gives a sense of community, of corporateness.

Those that showed a strong identification with their ethnic group motivated their sentiments with reference to the cultural meaning of ethnicity despite the political connotation it has gained. A man who spent time in prison after a political conviction spoke of his strong attachment to his homeland:

It is part of my being, my cultural upbringing. The richness of the language. I taught Sotho literature and wrote a drama that was used in schools. I visit there and speak Sotho at home. I'm torn between wanting to live there and the better developed areas where my other needs are met. All things being equal the traditional area is where I would live. I am not referring to the political sense. I deplore politically enforced ethnicity. My children speak Zulu to each other but we speak Sotho to them. They know they are Sotho. I'm African first then Sotho. I feel an attachment to Africa. P. W. Botha is rejecting me as a brother and thus rejecting himself as we are both Africans.

Others referred to the ethnic socialization of their children even though they speak English at home:

I feel a strong affiliation but not to the extent of being parochial about it. I'm proud of it. I differ with many people on it. It is sheer pretence to say being Xhosa is immaterial – deep down it does mean something. The same as a German or a Frenchman in South Africa would feel because of sheer numbers. We teach the children Shangaan. They learn Xhosa from their friends. I want my children to know they are Shangaan although they are really Xhosa. We go there [homeland of Gazankulu] in the holidays to show them their roots. We speak English at home but teach the children Shangaan. But ethnicity is irrelevant when one discusses the inclusion of Blacks in central government.

Ethnic extraction was valued as a conduit for a lifestyle, as was explained by a man who lives in his homeland:

I have a strong identification. The importance of ethnic extraction is that it has got the norms and traditions of my lifestyle. Once you cast yourself away from your ethnic group you find yourself in a no-man's-land.

The marital selection and language use of the elite as well as the meaning they attach to their ethnic heritage, suggest that these aspects of their traditionality follow the pattern noticed in respect of the rest of the African population, and weakens in the urban areas where people from different ethnic groups mingle and they are incorporated into the modern sector of society. There was no evidence that the elite are concerned with conserving their ethnic culture or that they attach any significance to perpetuating the purity of their language. They were, however, conscious of the politicization of ethnicity in the South African context and referred to the divisive effect of the policy of ethnic differentiation. They rejected ethnicity as legitimation for the political ordering of South Africa.

LOBOLA

The African custom best known to non-Africans is lobola, or brideswealth, erroneously seen to be the purchase of a wife. 'Lobola' is the Zulu form, with 'bogadi' the Sotho form, 'ikhazi' the Swazi form and 'thakha' the Venda form, although it has generally come to be known as lobola in English.

Traditionally[28] lobola is an important characteristic of marriage and involves the transfer of livestock, usually cattle, from the husband's to the wife's family. Although the accompanying verb 'pay' is used, in the sense that lobola is 'paid', the man never owns his wife as he would own property. She does not even become a member of his family and remains under the guardianship of her father's family. Besides being regarded as a bond between the respective families and

a sign of thankfulness towards the wife's family, lobola is an exchange
for the woman's potential to bear children. The woman enriches the
husband's family by the children she bears him in exchange he gives
the wife's family lobola. As such it is an agreement reached after
negotiation between representatives of the two families, providing
both families with equal advantages. Lobola is therefore related to
the husband's right to children and can be reclaimed if the woman is
barren. The father's social paternity is only settled when he finally
pays all the lobola agreed upon to his wife's family although the
marriage may have existed for many years. Livestock, mainly cattle,
usually serve as lobola, but goods and services can also be given. The
amount of lobola depends on the wealth of the man and the status of
the woman. The greater the lobola the higher the woman is honoured.
The whole lobola need not be paid at once and can be paid in
instalments, often as the wife bears children. The husband and his
relatives are responsible for lobola and the lobola received for a
daughter is often used to get a wife for a son, so that the same cattle
can move through many families cementing marriages along the way.
In modern times the nature and function of lobola have changed.
Changes that have been documented are the payment of lobola by
the husband himself instead of by his family, the replacement of
livestock by cash, an older age at marriage due to men having to work
to save money for lobola, the father of the bride keeping the whole
amount for himself thereby reducing the interest of the con-
sanguineal family in the union, and the perception of lobola as
compensating the bride's family for her upbringing and education. To
a certain extent lobola is still seen to have a stabilizing effect on
family life, as the wife's family has to return the lobola if she leaves
her husband, while the husband loses his lobola if his wife leaves him
because of ill-treatment. This leaves some scope for the two families
to become involved in the marriage.

More than four-fifths of the elite were married by the custom of
lobola, as is reflected by Table 5.7. This is less than the number of
marriages among their parents that included lobola, but more than
the actual or preferred number of lobola-marriages in respect of their
children. This shows that the preference for lobola-marriages has
decreased over the generations while that for Christian marriages has
increased.

The strength of a sentiment can often be tested by asking people
what they did or would do in a certain situation. This was done in
respect of lobola. The married elite were asked whether they had

Table 5.7   Marriage customs among the elite and their parents and
preference for their children

Marriage	Generation		
	Parents % (N)	*Elite* % (N)	*Children* % (N)
Lobola and Christian	80.4 (41)	80.7 (46)	40.4 (23)
Lobola only	15.7 (8)	1.8 (1)	–
Lobola and civil	–	–	1.8 (1)
Christian only	3.9 (2)	12.3 (7)	29.8 (17)
Civil only	–	5.3 (3)	3.5 (2)
Their choice	–	–	24.6 (14)
Total	100.0 (51)*	100.0 (57)	100.0 (57)†

*Nine had unmarried parents.
†Three of the elite never married.

Table 5.8   Expectation of lobola for daughters

Expectation of lobola	*Men* % (N)	*Women* % (N)	*Total* % (N)
No	39.6 (19)	66.7 (6)	43.9 (25)
Yes	47.9 (23)	–	40.4 (23)
Flexible	12.5 (6)	33.3 (3)	15.8 (9)
Total	100.0 (48)	100.0 (9)	100.0 (57)

expected lobola for their daughters, or would if they had daughters
(see Table 5.8). Less than half said they did/would not expect lobola,
while almost as many said they did/would expect it, while the rest
were flexible on the matter. None of the women expected lobola for
their children although a third were flexible on the issue. Almost half
of the men expected lobola for their daughters.

The younger members of the elite were more in favour of lobola
than the older members: a total of 48.1 per cent (13) of those younger
than 40 expected lobola for their daughters, compared with 33.3 per
cent (10) of those older than 40. This seems to confirm the resurgence
of interest in lobola among certain Africans, mentioned by the elite;
for example:

Among educated people it is not insisted upon. It is back again after it went out of fashion a few years ago. I'm sure I'd be influenced by the trend at the time that my daughters get married. I was sent to negotiate lobola for my brother. It nearly ended the marriage with all the conflict over money.

There was also evidence from the religious elite who are professionally involved in marital affairs that they encourage lobola. For example:

Yes, of course. I'd like her to marry in the context of those traditions. I don't care for the income. Lobola plays a role in involving the two families and making the process of getting married as difficult as possible. I expect it not for my sake but for the institution of marriage. It provides stability of marriage because it is then taken seriously. It is not a private thing but involves everyone who is interested in you. I hope the institution doesn't disappear. I am not impressed by anything that can replace it. Lobola is abused. These abuses have been brought about by the White people. In the beginning there was no fixed number of cattle. It was just a token. It became commercial when people came to work on the mines.

and

It is a good custom. It is saying that marriage is a communal thing. We see so many divorces because of the nuclear family in Western society. The lobola system is something people have misunderstood. Girls have no money value. It is wrong to talk of brideswealth. It means two families coming together to negotiate and involving many people. In the past people have even exchanged stones. It is not for the money.

Brideswealth was also found to be a common practice among the elites of tropical Africa where its social significance has changed. The sums of money offered are very large and are often used by the bride for furnishing her new home. Many a young man establishes his rights over his future spouse by paying her school fees.[29]

The religiosity of the elite played no role in their preference for or rejection of lobola although it did seem that geographical background played a role, as is evident from Table 5.9. Less people with

Table 5.9 Expectation of lobola for daughters according to the
background of the elite

Expectation of lobola	Rural background % (N)	Urban background % (N)	Total % (N)
No	47.4 (9)	42.1 (16)	43.9 (25)
Yes	42.1 (8)	39.5 (15)	40.4 (23)
Flexible	10.5 (2)	18.4 (7)	15.8 (9)
Total	100.0 (19)	100.0 (38)	100.0 (57)*

*Three people never married.

an urban background expected lobola for their daughters and more
of them were flexible on the issue than people with a rural background, indicating a weakening of traditional norms about lobola
among those with longer exposure to industrialization. This was also
noticed in Soweto.[30]

More people who identified with their ethnic extraction expected
lobola for their daughters than those who did not, as is evident from
Table 5.10, although there is no relationship between their ethnic
identification and the way their own marriage was formed.

Other studies have shown a strong attachment to lobola in urban
areas – even stronger than in rural areas. In Soweto, which is
generally regarded as accommodating the most educated Africans in
South Africa, it was found that 28.57 per cent were married by lobola
only, while 30.86 per cent were married by lobola as well as Christian

Table 5.10 Expectation of lobola for daughters according to ethnic
identification

Expectation of lobola	Ethnic identification	
	Important % (N)	Unimportant % (N)
No	37.5 (6)	46.3 (19)
Yes	56.3 (9)	34.1 (14)
Flexible	6.3 (1)	19.5 (8)
Total	100.0 (16)	100.0 (41)

Table 5.11   Views against lobola

Views against lobola	%	(N)
Too commercialized	48.0	(12)
Outdated/irrelevant	24.0	(6)
Couple need the money themselves	12.0	(3)
Parent didn't pay	8.0	(2)
Cause of divorce	4.0	(1)
Girls must be independent	4.0	(1)
Total	100.0	(25)

and civil ceremonies and 10.29 per cent by lobola and Christian ceremony.[31] In a larger survey it was found that 79.9 per cent of Soweto residents felt strongly that it was necessary to pay lobola, compared with 59.6 per cent of residents in Mabopane and Garankuwa near Pretoria, 64 per cent in Madadeni and Osizweni in Kwazulu and 46.8 per cent in Sibasa, the main town in Venda.[32] As many as 95 per cent of urban Xhosa in Port Elizabeth were in favour of lobola.[33] The relatively strong rejection of lobola by the elite in comparison with the general population of Soweto might possibly be explained by their high educational level. It has been pointed out that while the length of time a person spends in an urban area does not determine his adherence to a tribal custom such as lobola, a higher standard of education does seem to have an inhibiting effect.[34]

The 43.9 per cent (25) of the elite that were against lobola gave a number of reasons for their point of view, which are mostly related to the function of lobola in modern society. These are presented in Table 5.11.

The people who complained that lobola had become too commercialized mentioned their own experience. For example:

I don't expect it because of the experiences my wife and I went through. We were in debt for almost five years and started on a bad footing. It shouldn't happen to our daughters. We've decided both parents must invest something to kick them off in life equally. Call it a sophisticated kind of lobola.

Others complained that they were bound by custom:

It is a very difficult problem. If you don't ask for it you are seen as a
Black who has abandoned the custom that a wife is an asset who
can't be given free. I don't like the custom because it is a lower
concept in culture, like selling a daughter. It makes me feel
uncomfortable. We want to move up into a higher culture. Lobola
doesn't prevent divorce or separation. My first daughter got R350 –
I gave it back to her. The ceremony will be incomplete for the
relatives so we are bound by rituals and customs. It must just be
done that way.

The perception of lobola as placing a commercial value on children
created problems for others. For example:

No, I refused it. The custom has overstayed its welcome and
should be banished. It serves no purpose. A son is just as valuable.
It is wrong to say a daughter's value is demonstrated by lobola. The
man thinks he owns the woman and should return the money if the
marriage doesn't work. That is not what marriage is about. The
custom is exploited today.

and

I am dead against it. I thought I could break away from family and
African tradition but the family wouldn't let me be. They wouldn't
even allow me to negotiate. There is something in it that is not fair
in expecting a young man to pay as though his parents didn't
struggle to bring him up. The problem came when money replaced
beasts. With the money I got I bought my daughters furniture and
things to help them start off to give the young man a chance to start
off with something.

Others saw lobola as a cause of divorce:

In some cases it puts a lot of strain on the marriage. They use
lobola as an excuse for being wayward. It has lost its original
meaning and has become a primary cause of divorce. People
expect astronomical amounts like R4000 to R5000. In the traditional sense the money you get is used for setting up in life but
today parents just take the money and the newly marrieds have a
burden of debts. They have nothing to start life with. This is just

114   *The Modern African Elite of South Africa*

Table 5.12   Views in favor of lobola

Views in favor of lobola	%	(N)
Tradition	39.1	(9)
Tests a man	21.7	(5)
Binds two families	21.7	(5)
Ensures marital stability	8.7	(2)
Demonstrates wife's value	8.7	(2)
Total	100.0	(23)

where the conflict starts: I own you just as a piece of furniture. I would have no objections if it were used traditionally. Now it is causing problems.

Women referred to the effect of lobola on sex roles; for example:

I don't like it. My husband says it is not right not to accept lobola. He says it gives dignity to the affair as part of the family relationship/contract. I have conflict on it. It puts a burden on the boy and prejudices the girl, as the man may later force her to his will because he paid a lot for her.

and

It has died out in our family. Girls must be independent of their husband. If lobola is paid they must be subservient to their husband.

The 40.4 per cent (23) that were in favour of lobola cited tradition as their main argument, as is reflected in Table 5.12.

Traditional considerations dominated the arguments in favour of lobola. For example:

Of course I do. It is not an economic asset. It doesn't work like that. All customs are marvellous. People misinterpret them. It is just a token of appreciation and thanks for bringing up the wife and depriving the family of a daughter and wanting to compensate the family for it. Something we have struggled for we value. It doesn't matter how Christian or civilized, people still believe in the sanction of the ancestors and they will be distressed if the wife is not valued.

and

If you give away your daughter like that it causes bad luck. I asked for only R500 to test his sincerity and gave it back with more in furniture. I don't need his money but the custom is necessary.

and

Of course. I'm a Zulu. It is part of my culture. The husband must lobola. I may give her a house myself but the young man must lobola.

Family support was mentioned:

Lobola is something to unite two families as a means to hand over certain rights like authority, being the head of the family and the offspring taking the name of the family. Giving R50 is OK. The money is not important but what is important is to make sure that in the case of problems there is support.

The value of lobola in testing a man was also mentioned. For example:

I expect it very much. It has no ancestral attachment. It is not the tradition as much as something to strengthen the marriage bond. It is sign of commitment to each other. It shows my daughter will be something to him. It shows he is capable of saving and using money usefully. It shows me he can be a breadwinner, an assurance to me he is worthwhile.

Others would respect the feelings of the other family:

To see it as buying a wife would be misconstruing the situation. It is a good tradition binding two families who mediate in quarrels. In the case of my own daughters I will respect the man's decision. I would prefer it but won't be an obstacle if the man doesn't want to. It creates bonds between families forming them into a new unit.

Two women were also flexible on the issue:

> I really don't know. When I got married there was lobola. What w
> want is it as a formality but not the money, as others are makin
> out of it. They are asking R2000 to R3000. We as parents shouldn'
> force it. It should be a union of two people. If lobola has to come i
> will just be a formality. We won't make a big noise about it.

and

> The eldest was lobola-ed. It is like a play. You must keep up wit
> what is wanted. As an extended family person even I feel it is no
> important. The family feels the custom must be honoured. I am no
> sticky about it.

There is a clear division of views between those in favour of lobol
and those against it, while there is also an intergenerational decline i
the occurrence of lobola in favour of purely Christian marriage
Lobola seems to have lost some favour because of the commercia
connotation that has become attached to it in modern society. Ther
is, however, evidence of the modernization of lobola in that th
money received is returned to the couple in cash or in the form o
furniture. It then performs the same function as the assistance pa
rents in other Westernized societies give their newly married childre
to start them off in life.

ANCESTOR VENERATION

Traditionally[35] all the African tribes believe in an all-powerful super
natural being far removed from their daily existence. His presence i
known through impressive natural phenomena such as lightning
thunder, hail, rain, droughts and epidemics. There are also othe
lesser supernatural forces that live in mountains, forests and rivers
But the most important religious content of traditional culture lies i
the relationship between the living and the dead. During life every
one has two distinct parts – body and spirit. The spirit can depar
from the body during sleep or a faint. Death is the final separation o
the spirit from the body. The spirit then departs to the perfec
equivalent of earthly life where it has certain needs and maintains
social relationship with those left behind on earth. This is recipro

cated by the ceremonial veneration of ancestral spirits. The spirits have various ways of communicating with the living, and dreams are generally considered to be visits from the spirits. Veneration of the ancestral spirits is not a daily occurrence although they are kept in mind to avoid doing anything that would incur their wrath. Ancestral veneration is rather an occasional occurrence practised in times of crisis or if their blessing is required for safety or the success of a venture. It usually takes the form of offerings in which the male head of the household or family presides. The spirits are spoken to, thanked, beseeched or even reprimanded. The offerings take many forms including the presentation of beer, milk, food, tobacco and on important occasions the slaughtering of an animal, most often a goat, which is afterwards eaten. Women are sometimes excluded from these ceremonies.

The early missionaries tried to eradicate ancestral worship by presenting African followers with a choice between Christianity and traditional religion. As time went by, most churches accepted a synthesis between Christianity and traditional practices in which the Biblical concept of saints plays an important role. There are, however, still churches, notably those that arose from Afrikaner missionary activity, that require followers to forsake traditional religious practices. The majority of contemporary Africans belong to an orthodox church although many of them have broken ties with formal churches because of the seeming inability of these churches to effect social change. There is strong evidence of a recent resurgence of ancestor worship among young Africans, probably a manifestaion of the upsurge of Black Consciousness and its concomitant assertion of African culture patterns.[36] Customs such as ancestor veneration have also been found to have a political significance in a Pan-Africanist context as being 'consciously used to foster the sense of a broad common identity of Bantu-speaking and other African people as a pressure-group in a Western political system'.[37]

The majority of the elite, namely 71.7 per cent (43), honoured the spirits of their ancestors, while 28.3 per cent (17) did not believe spirits existed, as is reflected by Table 5.13.

As is shown by Table 5.14, the degree to which the elite venerated the spirits of their ancestors was not related to whether or not they identified with their ethnic extraction.

Education did, however, seem to play some role. The better-educated elite venerated the spirits of their ancestors to a lesser extent than did those with less education, as is reflected in Table 5.15.

Table 5.13   Ancestor veneration displayed by the elite

Ancestor veneration	Men %	(N)	Women %	(N)	Total %	(N)
None: they don't exist	28.0	(14)	30.0	(3)	28.3	(17)
Inactive	30.0	(15)	20.0	(2)	28.3	(17)
Active	42.0	(21)	50.0	(5)	43.3	(26)
Total	100.0	(50)	100.0	(10)	100.0	(60)

Table 5.14   Ancestor veneration according to ethnic identification

Ethnic identification	Ancestor veneration					
	None %	(N)	Inactive %	(N)	Active %	(N)
Important	29.4	(5)	35.3	(6)	26.9	(7)
Unimportant	70.6	(12)	64.7	(11)	73.1	(19)
Total	100.0	(17)	100.0	(17)	100.0	(26)

Table 5.15   Ancestor veneration according to education

Ancestor veneration	Education			
	School %	(N)	Post-school %	(N)
None: they don't exist	18.2	(2)	30.6	(15)
Inactive	–		34.7	(17)
Active	81.8	(9)	34.7	(17)
Total	100.0	(11)	100.0	(49)

This is supported by other research which found that 39.4 per cent of educated urban Africans in professional and other trained occupations do not believe in ancestor veneration, compared with only 11.7 per cent among uneducated people.[38]

The younger members of the elite venerated the spirits of their ancestors to a greater extent than did the older members of the elite,

Table 5.16   Ancestor veneration according to age

Ancestor veneration	Younger than 40 % (N)	Older than 40 % (N)	Total % (N)
None: they don't exist	18.2 (2)	30.6 (15)	28.3 (17)
Inactive	36.4 (4)	26.5 (13)	28.3 (17)
Active	45.5 (5)	42.9 (21)	43.3 (26)
Total	100.0 (11)	100.0 (49)	100.0 (60)

as is evident from Table 5.16. This unexpected finding might be explained by the upsurge in Black Consciousness among young Africans which rejects White values and asserts African culture patterns.[39]

When one looks at the background of the elite (Table 5.17), it is evident that those with an urban background venerated the spirits of their ancestors to a greater extent than those with a rural background. This accords with research reported in 1983 that 57 per cent of urban males attended veneration ceremonies in the city, compared with 36 per cent who never attended such ceremonies, and 7 per cent who attended ceremonies in a traditional area.[40] In a broader survey it was found that 75.7 per cent of Soweto residents paid tribute to their ancestors, compared with 51.4 per cent in Mabopane and Garankuwa near Pretoria, 79.4 per cent in Madadeni and Osizweni in Kwazulu, and 21.3 per cent in Sibasa in Venda.[41] In Central America belief in magic and protective charms against witchcraft were reported to be more frequent in the towns than in rural areas.[42]

The elite who came from families that had lived in the city for a longer period venerated the spirits of their ancestors to a greater

Table 5.17   Ancestor veneration according to background

Ancestor veneration	Rural background % (N)	Urban background % (N)
None	35 (7)	25 (10)
Inactive	35 (7)	25 (10)
Active	30 (6)	50 (20)
Total	100 (20)	100 (40)

Table 5.18   Ancestor veneration according to city generation

Ancestor veneration	City generation					
	1st % (N)		2nd % (N)		3rd % (N)	
None	43.5	(10)	23.1	(6)	–	
Inactive	30.4	(7)	23.1	(6)	50.0	(3)
Active	26.1	(6)	53.8	(14)	50.0	(3)
Total*	100.0	(23)	100.0	(26)	100.0	(6)

*Five did not live in a city.

extent that those who had a closer generational attachment to a rural environment, as is evident from Table 5.18.

The veneration of ancestral spirits by urbanized people might be a result of the insecurity of city life, as was suggested by a church leader:

There is confusion in the community. When people don't have social, economic and political security they try anything that might work. It is like trying their luck. There is more syncretism here than in rural areas. There are more pressures here than in a typical rural area and they say they honour them but they are really only grasping for security.

There also seemed to be a relationship between religiosity and ancestor veneration. As is evident from Table 5.19, 68 per cent (34) of the elite that attended church services honoured their ancestors.

Table 5.19   Ancestor veneration according to religiosity

Ancestor veneration	Attendance at religious services					
	Regularly/ sometimes % (N)		Seldom/ never % (N)		Total % (N)	
None: they don't exist	32.0	(16)	10.0	(1)	28.3	(17
Inactive	30.0	(15)	20.0	(2)	28.3	(17
Active	38.0	(19)	70.0	(7)	43.3	(26
Total	100.0	(50)	100.0	(10)	100.0	(60

Table 5.20   Attitude to lobola according to ancestor veneration

Attitude to lobola	Ancestor veneration		
	Disbelief % (N)	Inactive % (N)	Active % (N)
Expected	33.3 (5)	6.3 (1)	38.5 (10)
Not expected	33.3 (5)	62.5 (10)	50.0 (13)
Flexible	33.3 (5)	31.3 (5)	11.5 (3)
Total*	100.0 (15)	100.0 (16)	100.0 (26)

*Only married people included.

while 90 per cent (9) of those that did not go to church honoured them. The ancestors are often seen as intermediaries between man and God. The worship of ancestors is not separated from the worship of God and a good relationship with the ancestors means a good relationship with God. Ancestors and Christ as the two channels of intercession with God used separately and together in times of crisis, are accepted by many formal churches. There are, however, churches that totally reject the concept of ancestral spirits.[43] It follows that ancestor veneration and religiosity are not necessarily mutually exclusive.

It is interesting to note that 40 per cent (6) of the religious elite believed that the spirits of their ancestors exist while 13.3 per cent (2) honoured them actively. They were obviously affiliated to churches that condone ancestral veneration. Even more interesting is that 93.3 per cent of the professionals with their high level of education believed these spirits exist, while half of them were active in their veneration.

When one compares the occurrence of ancestor veneration with the elite's views on lobola, as is done in Table 5.20, it seems that there is no convergence between the veneration of the spirits of ancestors and the expectation of lobola for their daughters. In fact, more people that honoured their ancestors rejected lobola than did those that did not believe in ancestral spirits.

The elite that believed the spirits of their ancestors exist, honoured them in various ways. Details are presented in Table 5.21.

The high proportion of the elite that slaughtered beasts or attended slaughterings, namely 24, or 40 per cent of the total sample, is not exceptional if one considers other findings. In 1981 it was found that 85.8 per cent of Soweto residents felt that an animal should be

Table 5.21   Method of ancestral veneration

Ancestor veneration	Occurrence %	(N)
Slaughters himself	34.9	(15)
Attends family slaughters	20.9	(9)
Believes they exist but does nothing	18.6	(8)
Honours them by remembrance	16.3	(7)
Visits graves	4.7	(2)
Prayers	2.3	(1)
Death rites	2.3	(1)
Total	100.0	(43)*

*Seventeen did not venerate the spirits of their ancestors.

slaughtered when a close relative passes away. The comparative figures for Mabopane and Garankuwa near Pretoria are 61.9 per cent, for Madadeni and Osizweni in Kwazulu 79.9 per cent and for Sibasa in Venda 38.7 per cent.[44] In 1965 it was found that 54.29 per cent of Soweto residents approached their ancestors by slaughtering an animal while they were in an urban area.[45]

The elite that honoured the spirits of their ancestors by slaughtering, regarded it as part of their tradition; for example:

> I give a little do for them. The family gets together and we slaughter once a year. I regularly call them back in my mind and respect them for me being here. Some traditions must be kept and others thrown out. Lobola and ancestors must be kept as good traditions. We must keep the best of all worlds we know and build an even better world.

Veneration also strengthened relationships with relatives out of town; for example:

> Every year we have a ceremony. When the family can get together after the harvest I organize with my uncles at Louis Trichardt and we have a ceremony. Before eating anything of the harvest we celebrate. We make African beer and there is African dancing. Most of my paternal line is here in town. I buy a goat and slay it and buy beer so that we can also celebrate in town.

The role that ancestors play in daily life emerged in various interviews. For example:

I slaughter a beast to thank them for the good that has come to my family. At weddings we appeal to them and we just generally appeal to them for assistance. I consider myself to be under their wing in a sense.

One drew a parallel between ancestral spirits and Christ:

I slaughter goats and talk to them. One has got to remember them sometimes. The Christ we believe in also rose from the dead. All religious people believe it.

The value their family placed on slaughtering was also mentioned; for example:

Ancestral beliefs are so interwoven into our life that you find yourself in one with the other showing respect. I play a role indirectly. In our family we name children after ancestors. We slaughter at weddings. I don't believe much in that but it is part of life in a community where it is the norm. I do it at funerals too, otherwise the relatives would complain. Then at the unveiling of tombstones we put a stone or soil on the grave. I also visit their graves. My father died while I was on the [Robben] Island and later the family took me to his grave. I prayed to my father after my brother had addressed him saying 'Here he is.'

Acceding to family wishes was important:

Yes, I remember them. We ask for a special mass for my father – we can do that in the Roman Catholic Church – and we slaughter at parties. In my own belief system I don't believe slaughtering does anything but I must respect my broader family in this. I go along for their peace of mind. They are an important support to me so I can't reject their custom. There was a ceremony at the birth of my children to obtain the blessing of the ancestors. It had to be done for the sake of the family.

The high cost of obtaining a beast to slaughter was mentioned many times:

I honour them mostly in prayer. I haven't slaughtered on my own but would do so if I had the means. At parties and weddings we slaughter. We combine with others and share costs. I like doing it.

Some churches have incorporated ancestral veneration into their doctrine while others reject it completely. Two religious leaders explained:

I honour them very much. They are people who are saints. I am very fond of them. The Book of Hebrews says we are surrounded by saints and they are part of them. I don't slaughter goats or any other visible form of honour. I serve them as saints not in a tangible way. I also expect them to bless me. I believe what I get I get from them.

and:

When my father was alive we had an annual ritual which was beautiful. I miss it now. Once in a while I go and talk to my father at his grave. I find it very soothing. I venerate my ancestors but don't regard them as taking the place of Christ. They are intermediaries but don't replace Christ. One must make a distinction between good and bad ancestors and serve the good ones.

A religious leader from one of the churches that rejected ancestral veneration complained of its effect on the community:

It is difficult to become a committed Christian if one believes in ancestors. One never knows what the medicine men prescribe. You are asked to offer prayers to their forefathers, slaughter beasts and so serve a host of idolatrous gods. It worries me to see how people are hounded and haunted by these things. I am completely liberated from it.

The perception of ancestors as a refuge emerged in many interviews. For example:

I do believe in a life here-after where they will be. When I am really upset and down and out I appeal to those that might hear. It is also a good kind of custom to tell children: 'Don't behave like that because they are watching.'

and: 'When I am in trouble I honour everyone and try anything.'

Others remembered their ancestors without formal veneration; for example:

> I honour my father by being proud of him. I don't slaughter, although the tradition is coming back. I never knew it in my home. I am against it because my father never did it. He was a strong churchman who never participated in any customary rites.

Some people expressed a perception that ancestral worship was not part of a modern lifestyle; for example:

> I am completely alienated from that outlook on life. My family also reject it. I stay away when the extended family does these things.

It is evident from the analysis that more than two-thirds of the elite believed their ancestors existed in spiritual form while many initiated ceremonies to honour them. This seems to indicate that their modernity has not eradicated their traditional religion. Instead, elements of their traditional religion have been incorporated into modern Christian religious observance. This is underlined by the fact that the younger elite as well as those with an urban background were more active in their veneration than those with a rural background, although the lesser-educated people were slightly more active in their veneration than the higher-educated ones.

CONCLUSION

Evidence on the elite's practice of traditional customs supports the thesis stated at the beginning of this chapter that modernity and traditionality are not mutually exclusive. Some elements of traditionality seem to decline in the modern environment while others persist. In this, the elite reflect the pattern already noticed in the broader African community. Most of them did not identify with their specific ethnic extraction and the longer they were exposed to an urban environment the less they did so. The absence of an interest in the preservation of ethnic identity as reflected in marital selection and the use of vernacular languages seems to suggest that specific ethnic identification disappears when it is not supported by geographic isolation, legislation or mobilization by charismatic leaders. The culture patterns of the various ethnic groups are in any case very similar, and cultural distinctions between groups appear to merge into one broad African culture. The elite also drew a clear distinction between the importance they attach to their ethnicity and the government's use of ethnicity in the political ordering of South Africa, which they rejected. The customs of lobola and ancestor veneration persist in the elite and consequently seem to be functional in modern African society. There are indications that lobola and ancestor veneration have been adapted to the modern environment. The evidence that the practices of lobola and ancestor veneration do not overlap suggests that the two customs have different functions and that their occurrence cannot be regarded as symptomatic of a traditional orientation. These conclusions are important, as the elite are indisputably modern, sophisticated people. Attempts to use the occurrence of traditional customs as an indicator of relative modernism/traditionalism or in indices of Westernization are therefore completely invalid.

6 Socio-Political Orientations

Elite studies are usually undertaken to illuminate the power structure of a society. As such they produce insights into the lifestyle and values of leaders as well as the social processes in that society. Even in communities that are excluded from institutionalized political processes, as is the case of the Africans in South Africa, elites are none the less opinion-leaders who represent the experience and expertise in that community. As was shown in the preceding chapters, the African elites described here are, on the one hand, leaders in a wide range of fields for which they are highly qualified and appropriately rewarded, while, on the other, they display a strong solidarity with the rest of the African community. This indicates that they play an active, innovative role and that their views would influence opinion in the African community.

The critical issue regarding Africans in South Africa is their inclusion in the societal community. The elite's orientation to this is the theme of this chapter. The aspects that are analysed are African exclusion, potential political leadership of a new South Africa, White fears and the maintenance of the free enterprise economic system. The analysis represents their views at the middle of 1985 before the first declaration of a state of emergency.

AFRICAN EXCLUSION

Historical factors are responsible for the exclusion of Africans from the societal community. In recent years reaction to this has increased conflict threatening the stability of South African society. This has in turn led to recognition by the government of the need for a reconstitution of societal structures to include Africans. All of the elite in this study recognized African exclusion as the crucial problem facing South Africa. This was expressed as follows:

Black feeling is very, very bitter. They are not happy about the tricameral system excluding them. They regard the Coloureds as their offspring and the Indians as foreigners. The new constitution is seen as a way of forming a power bloc against Blacks. This is the crux of the problem in South Africa. Blacks want the fourth chamber.

While most of the elite simply referred to the problem as 'apartheid', others referred to it in terms of powersharing, Black anger, White fears, radicalism and the distribution of wealth and education. Many referred to multiple factors; for example:

> The biggest problem is our obsession with race and the divisions that that kind of racialism has engendered. Then there is the matter of the incalculable human and material resources we have wasted. Australia has a population of only seventeen million people and has a gross national product four times that of South Africa. South Africa has spent half its lifetime so that 75 percent of its population is denied economic participation and education and made hostages to the policy of apartheid. We must release our tremendous resources – human and mineral – and free the Black man so that his intelligence and productivity can be used to the advantage of the whole country.

They were all concerned about the conflict in South Africa, which they related to the political system. For example:

> The uncertainty about the future affects everyone in the country – Black and White. What will become of South Africa next year, even in the distant future? It is very negative this uncertainty. Who will live in South Africa? Will people live? How many will survive with the riots? When one dies many others die – their offspring. Young people die in great numbers – Black and White. Who will be left? The cause is ignorance and greed and a fear of the unknown. The solution is to scrap the legalized part of it and bring people together. Then gradually we will get a solution. The problem in South Africa is legalized apartheid. If it were scrapped altogether little will change but the barriers between people will start to break down.

There was also unanimity on the underlying cause of the conflict – the political system – although there was an incredulity about the way that the conflict manifested, especially the reaction of young people. For example:

> What bugs me is the attitude of young Blacks at the moment. I don't understand their attitude. Mandela and Sobukwe showed themselves as leaders and never stood back. Today, groups stand back and hide and try to direct affairs and create violence. These so-called leaders see violence and stayaways as a success, but in the meantime people have lost their wages and have walked miles, but the firms they work for still exist as before. It doesn't make sense. The destruction of vehicles also worries me. It hurts innocent people. When I try to discuss it with my son he says, 'Dad, you don't understand.'

In a differentiated society where the polity has a high level of legitimacy and the political process attends to the needs of that society, political activity is relegated to the political sub-system and only becomes salient to broader society when elections are held. This is largely the case in the White community. In the African community, where there is no institutionalized political sub-system and all matters pertaining to Africans are decided by Whites in such a way that there is a very low level of legitimacy for the ordering of society in the African community, all sub-systems have become politicized. This has had the effect that in whatever sphere of life Africans move, they are confronted by the effects of the government's political ideology. From its opinion surveys the Buthelezi Commission found that political concerns are ranked among the most prominent life interests in the Black population as a whole. Among a number of significant groups, such as those with higher education and the people who are most discontent with life, political concerns tend to over-shadow all others.[1] The extent of this became evident when the elite discussed problems in their fields of activity. In the legal field, where Africans are completely excluded from law-making, the following evaluation was made:

> South Africa's courts still reflect the racist situation. Black ac-cuseds are entirely lost in White courts. Most accuseds are Blacks judged by Whites. In South Africa we have a White man's justice and the Black man's battle against that justice. There are enough Blacks who can be used in the administration of the law. There are some 250 Black lawyers but more must be produced. Most politicians

are drawn from the legal profession. We must stimulate the Black legal profession. We need more and better law schools. We don't need racialism in law schools or even in universities. Black lawyers must get the best university education available in the country. The ideal situation is impossible with bush universities. Legal education for Blacks is not the same as for Whites. One just has to compare the legal library at the University of the North to the one at the University of the Witwatersrand to see this.

The unequal distribution of income, service benefits such as medical aid and health resources were mentioned in the medical field:

> My work depends on a patient's ability to pay. It breaks my heart that patients can't pay for the drugs I would sometimes like to prescribe. We need a prepaid medical insurance scheme. Britain's is my model although there is criticism of it. In particular, preventive medicine must be available to all. We see far too many diseases which are a result of the political situation, such as malnutrition and cholera, which didn't exist when I was a student. The government refuses to make clean water available to all areas. One must attend to all living conditions and all environments to make these diseases extinct.

The institution of national states and independent homelands affects nursing:

> When we want to discuss national nursing issues, the nurses who are citizens of the national states and work in South Africa are told that they can't make a contribution because they don't have full membership rights in the South African Nursing Association.

The differential education system affects the supply of skills and was mentioned by an educationalist:

> There must be equal opportunities. We must give every educable child in the country the opportunity to attain equal levels with Whites. A compulsory system must be introduced. They must then have the opportunity to sell their labour on the market in an equal way. White education has a philosophy, namely Christian nationalism. Black education has no philosophy, which means that it is for inanimate beings. Black and White education should be part of the

same system. Children get no preparation for life with the confusion in schools and education. Our own institutions are poor in quality, while the White institutions which have facilities to turn out well-skilled Blacks still exclude Blacks.

In religion, Christianity was equated with White domination, as a religious leader explained:

Speaking as a Black growing up in the jungle of Africa, we knew God, not Christ. When Christ was brought to us some of us accepted Christ. But it soon became evident that the same people who brought Christ are not living Christians. To many people Christianity is taken to be a White man's religion. When they see what Whites do, they query whether God is for everyone. If God is for everyone why can't there be justice for everyone? We must explain that where God is, the devil also is. It is very difficult for us. The young people are now rejecting Christianity.

The exclusion of Africans from full participation in the free enterprise system was seen to retard initiative, as an entrepreneur explained:

I cannot get money. I can't raise the loans I need because I can't give security like a White man would because I cannot own land. The whole system is just terrible. I say this because I know how it feels to be outside South Africa. How you think – this thing that is called the mind is a difficult thing because once you are outside and you are in a free situation you find yourself being more intelligent than you were before. Whatever you think about . . . when you look at a glass you think: How can I make glasses? whereas in our situation it is useless to think of it. Nobody is going to allow me to manufacture glasses. In that way you don't have initiative and innovation.

A sports administrator pointed out that there was not yet equality in sport:

The biggest problem is mistrust between Blacks and Whites. Blacks have no facilities, while Whites have all. White sport is commercialized, so they have the means. It makes competition unfair. We are trying to form a foundation to uplift sport in the townships. Another problem is in administration. Whites want to lead. They don't want to accept Blacks. It doesn't matter who leads if he has sport at heart. Whites have gymnasiums to which they don't want to admit Blacks. City councils still exercise power over sports fields and won't share them. Then they say our sport is non-racial.

Artists complained that they do not get adequate recognition, because they are Black:

Even in art there is apartheid. Art education is bad. In the fifties when Black artists started to emerge they were written off as township artists and their work called township art. It was very disparaging and caused a lot of harm to what is produced by Black artists. Their work is derogated and it has discouraged artists to a great extent. For example, I am a landscape painter but always include houses and people. It is called township art. If a White paints the same thing it is just art. Whites then get better prices for their art just because they are White.

The unanimous solution presented by the elite was the reconstitution of the political system. This was seen to be beneficial to everyone in the country; for example:

Politics. Everything revolves around that. If we could get politics right, we would have a superpower. If we could give everyone who is talented an opportunity, we would go far. With our minerals we would be a superpower.

There was, however, difference of opinion on how a new socio-political system could be achieved.

In reaction to the increased conflict in the country since the implementation of the 1983 constitution, the government conceded that its homeland policy as the chief instrument for African political expression had been unsuccessful, and declared that means would be sought to include Africans in central democratic political institutions. Up to the middle of 1988, the only development in this direction has been the publication of a bill envisaging the establishment of a multiracial advisory council to consider a new constitution which would make provision for the inclusion of Africans in democratic political structures. A variety of measures have in the meantime been implemented to reduce formal racial discrimination which have relieved specific grievances, notably the abolition of influx control in the middle of 1986. This approach of the government to implement reform incrementally elicited comments such as the following:

> We must demytholize race; take race out of the constitution. Then people will find a way of living together. If we abolish the Group Areas Act forthwith, nothing will happen. Then why carry the racist stigma? Blacks won't move to Houghton and Killarney. They will certainly move to Johannesburg as traders, because that is where Blacks spend their money. If a child wants to come to school in Soweto why stop him? The reform process is done by fits and starts and to make it easier to live within the system. Blacks don't accept that system.

The majority of the elite felt that political change would have to be fundamental to satisfy African aspirations. None of them unconditionally thought that a socio-political system acceptable to Africans could incrementally be evolved out of the present system. This was sometimes expressed very strongly; for example:

> Existing structures must be destroyed. A national convention must create new structures which no one fears. You mustn't try and reform already bad structures. You must start completely anew and call a national convention, get leaders out of jail, get Oliver Tambo back and discuss the construction of a new constitution for South Africa. You can't equate what is evil with what is good. You can't evolve something good out of what is evil.

A little less than a third (32.8 percent, or 19) of the elite felt that a suitable political system could be incrementally evolved provided that certain conditions were met. More than two-thirds (67.2 percent, or 39), however, felt that the existing political structures should be abandoned and new ones devised. Age was the only factor found to play a role in the elite's perception of how change should be implemented. As is evident from Table 6.1, more people over the age of fifty than those younger than fifty thought a system acceptable to Africans could be evolved if certain conditions were met, although they were still very much in the minority. Reasons for their preference for radical change centred around a mistrust of the government and impatience. This was expressed as follows:

Table 6.1   Acceptability of incremental reform according to age

Age group	Acceptability of reform					
	No % (N)		Conditional yes % (N)		Total % (N)	
Twenties	100.0	(1)	–		100.0	(1)
Thirties	77.8	(7)	22.2	(2)	100.0	(9)
Forties	88.2	(15)	11.8	(2)	100.0	(17)
Subtotal 20–49	85.2	(23)	14.8	(4)	100.0	(27)
Fifties	50.0	(12)	50.0	(12)	100.0	(24)
Sixties	57.1	(4)	42.9	(3)	100.0	(7)
Subtotal 50–69	51.6	(16)	48.4	(15)	100.0	(31)
Total	67.2	(39)	32.8	(19)	100.0	(58)*

*Information is not available in respect of two respondents.

We must start again. The oppressed won't accept apartheid even if it is deodorized. If P. W. Botha definitely demonstrated he wants to negotiate on a new South Africa on the will of the majority, he will still find an audience. But time is running out. Blacks are becoming more and more suspicious of P. W. He must release Mandela, recall the exiles and stop the Bantustans. The government will really need to be trusted first. It will not be trusted by the Blacks until it opens the doors and recognises the Black political parties now banned. The government has nothing to lose if it recognises the ANC. It can deal with the bad aspects [i.e. the violent tendencies] separately and not act against the whole organization. That will be positive change. We don't know about them because we don't give them a chance to come to the light. I could propagate communism because I don't know anything about it.

Changes that had taken place were seen as inconsequential; for example:

It may have been possible five or ten years ago. Right now the feelings and perceptions have so shifted that people realise the basic structures have to change. For us to really get Black people to accept the new product it will have to be totally different, to be sure it won't be the old wine put into new bottles. You can't continue with the same concept of the government of the townships the way it is. People are totally disenchanted with it. What you must do is to overhaul it completely and be able to convince people that the fact that they live in townships is a historical mistake. It should never have been that way. It should have been the way it was before the government stepped in. In places like Lady Selbourne we had White, Black, Coloured and Indian, Chinese, the whole lot living together and it worked. People didn't have hang-ups about this and the other. The government actually has been the perpetrator of the wrongs we are dealing with in South Africa. They emphasized the differences that made people mistrust one another. So I don't think we can have a new social order by simply going on with the structures the way they are. We will have to change them drastically.

The slow rate of change was blamed for the violence in the country; for example:

It depends on the White rulers whether there will be violence. People are giving their lives to the country and more and more are prepared to do so. People are looking to violence. The government has led the people to believe they must be pressurized into change. The government has put itself into a weak position. It started with the '76 riots. They wait until there is a problem before they act.

The prospect of a national conflagration is very real to the general African community. The Buthelezi Commission found that upward of 98 percent of the various groups of males interviewed said spontaneously that bloodshed, internal war or revolution would result if the government introduced no changes in the lives of Africans within ten years. The report refers to the emergence of a political culture in which violence is easily articulated, and adds that revolution is no longer the topic only of frustrated intellectuals and armchair radicals.[2]

The problem of legitimacy was recognized as an underlying issue in relations between Africans and the government; for example:

We must start anew. Things must simmer down and then we must get around a table and start from scratch. The government is thinking for the Black people and this is unacceptable because the people are not involved. The government doesn't know what the people need and want. For example, someone in government decided a youth camp should be set for the supposed youth leaders. The people involved with the youth were ignored. The whole thing failed because the children weren't interested in the content of the course. The government is making the same mistake in politics. The repeal of things like the Mixed Marriages Act is a minor. Blacks and Whites should be brought together to get to know each other and break down barriers.

The nineteen people that felt an acceptable system could be evolved out of present structures, mentioned three preconditions for successful change: that legitimate African leaders be involved, the prior removal of all formal racial differentiation, and that the government convince Africans that it was serious about change by acting as fast as possible. The necessity of involving accepted leaders was explained as follows:

> There must be negotiation with the real leaders – the people who are respected by their people – to find out what they want. The ANC, PAC, even Inkatha – they must all be included. The problem of the government is that it chooses what people to call leaders.

The problem of legitimacy was also seen to be compounded by the poverty of the African community when the possibility of successful change was considered. For example:

> A lot has to do with the socio-economic status of Blacks. If you give Blacks a better deal which will restore their dignity it is possible to envisage that under such conditions a political system that suits Whites and Blacks can be evolved. As long as Blacks are regarded as third-class citizens and their opportunities for full participation in the economy of the country are restricted by laws and other artificial barriers, it will be impossible to evolve a political system which will be moderate.

and:

> We've got to help Blacks improve their socio-economic standard of

living. At the moment Whites are on top and it is important to bring Blacks up the sooner the better. But is must be done by Blacks. There are problems now because too many things are done by Whites, and Blacks don't have a share in what is done. Local councils don't work because the government is still doing the thinking for them. Blacks must be seen to do things for themselves, but that doesn't mean Blacks at their own discretion shouldn't be able to approach Whites for expertise. Blacks must run all things for Blacks and get together for things of mutual concern.

There was evidence that political developments in other African countries, especially those bordering on South Africa, are followed keenly in the African community. Many referred to the 'holocaust' that was predicted for Zimbabwe after the adoption of majority rule – a 'holocaust' which did not materialize – and to the fact that there are now more Whites in Africa than during colonial times. For example:

Whites are scared the Blacks will do to them what they are doing to Blacks. As in Swaziland I'd show that we won't do to Whites what they do to us. They are gradually forgetting colour. There was perhaps more apartheid in Swaziland than here. Blacks had to buy through windows, but since the takeover by Blacks there have been no Whites leaving the country. The fears that Whites are having can only be allayed if the Whites now change their attitudes. Let me make an example of Zimbabwe. If Smith [the last White prime minister] was not as stubborn as he was, the relationship between Black and White would not have been strained to the extent that it was. If he had seen the symptoms and changed in time before so many people were bitter . . . I happen to have been in Zimbabwe when Mugabe came back from the bush. He said, 'We are fighting the system not the colour. Now that we have done away with the system let us start a new life. Let us forget the past.' It has not been easy from the Black side. He is seen by the Black people as someone who is too forgiving. But he is actually succeeding because most of the Whites that went away are going back.

The occurrence of inter-tribal tensions in other countries and its relevance for South Africa was often discussed:

We must start from scratch and break down barriers between

ethnic groups and racial groups. We are building up to a Zimbabwe situation where the Shonas fight the Matabeles. This is where Inkatha is leading us. We were rising above this, when the present system came along to sharpen barriers, as in the new tricameral system.

The elite were very strong in their feeling that government policies exacerbated these tensions. For example:

If South Africa were governed by one tribe we would have the same problem as Zimbabwe, where the problem is a clash between the Shonas and the Matabeles. Such a possibility has been created by this very government that wanted to divide and rule created tribes.The problem will be solved by one national leader who is respected by all, like Nelson Mandela.

Although the issue was not explored, some had concrete ideas about a system that would be acceptable to Africans. After a unitary system, the idea of a federal system was the most popular and illustrates the elite's identification with other groups in the country as well as their perception of a common loyalty to South Africa. A federation was motivated as follows:

I would agree it would be less problematic to evolve a system that accommodates some aspects of the existing order. For example, I would not completely dismantle the homelands as they are constituted. What I would do is to build upon them so that they become provinces, additional provinces of a federal structure. In other words, they don't have to be completely dissolved. What we will do is perhaps change the system of electing leaders in our homelands. Instead of basing it entirely on the institution of chieftainship, I would prefer to look at something more sustainable than just the system of chiefs. Some sort of merit. We've got boys at the University of the North doing political science and they are aspiring to lead their people. We cannot relegate such people to a subordinate role just because they don't have blue blood in their veins. I think we must look for a more equitable system and transform them into provinces, not into independent states because they would never be recognised internationally. That leads to a lot of embarrassment, not only for the leaders there but for South Africa that produced them. So it is something that needs to be attended to very quickly, because if this frustration builds up it could also bring about long-term instability in the homelands for the leadership there. We need a federal structure but, having said that, at the top we would certainly need everybody there. Each constituency would have the right to vote a certain number of people into the federal parliament. They would exercise some kind of local democratic vote. That would entitle them to bring people into a federal structure. That would perhaps be a system that would bring us the least possible conflict, because it would accommodate a number of existing structures that already are there. But if we want to start from scratch and demolish everything, we are going to find it extremely difficult to bring along a lot of existing leaders of the country. The government will eventually have to convene a meeting. A meeting of minds. Black. White. Everybody. All the interested groups must meet to discuss the road ahead and put forward the salient concerns – what we are to start with in structuring a common South African society. We may have to start with a constitution. First of all we've got to evolve a workable, acceptable constitution, and having done that, we must throw it around for the people to comment on, and later we could come together to amend it accordingly and implement it. This seems to be the logical way of going about it in my mind.

Thus, among the African elite there is a unanimous rejection of the ideology of separation and a strong claim for inclusion in the socio-political system of a unitary state.

POLITICAL LEADERSHIP

Opportunities for meaningful political leadership in the African community have until now been restricted to traditional hereditary structures in the homelands. People have been elected to local authorities but with very low percentage polls, indicating community rejection of the (separate) local government system, while others have become leaders of national political organizations but without being able to demonstrate their strength in elections. At the same time, there are indications that prominent people are waiting to enter politics in the modern sector when what they consider to be meaningful opportunities arise. (A number of the elite also said that they would be interested in becoming politicians in a new South Africa.) All this has had the result that little is known about the kind of

Table 6.2   Personal qualities desired of a leader

Quality	%	(N)
Non-racial/non-ethnic	56.7	(34)
Accommodating	43.3	(26)
Compassion	33.3	(20)
Decisive statesman	33.3	(20)
Democratic/unprejudiced	31.7	(19)
Teambuilder believing in everyone's ability	21.7	(13)
Humility	15.0	(9)
Practising Christian	11.7	(7)
Well-educated	10.0	(6)
Trustworthy and honest	10.0	(6)
Businessman/economist	3.3	(2)
Discretion	1.7	(1)

political leader the modernized African community prefers, which is important if one considers the size of the African community and that their leaders will play a prominent role in any system in which they are included. Being leaders in their own right, the elite are more able than most to articulate the political leadership values of the African community.

The elite's choice of leader displayed their emphasis on a just and democratic system. There was a strong feeling that a fully democratic system would produce the right person. The qualities the elite would like to see in the leader of a new South Africa are presented in Table 6.2. More than half of them regarded a non-racial and non-ethnic disposition to be the most important quality required.

Although most of them had firm ideas about the kind of personality that was required, it was also pointed out that a leader was the product of a system and that a democratic system was a prerequisite for the emergence of an appropriate person; for example:

A government is not a person but the people themselves. The leader is only a figurehead that does what most people want. P. W. Botha has done his best but can't do more than what others let him do. It is ridiculous to speak of an ideal person. The people dictate. If he acts alone he'll be kicked out. What we need is a new system where there are only people who live in one country.

The unstable political conditions were seen as an obstacle to the emergence of a suitable leader. The conflict was seen to be too advanced and extensive to allow anyone to lead the country success- fully. For example:

> It will be very, very difficult to get an ideal person out of South Africa. Whites have so much to lose because of their selfishness. Blacks have so many scores to settle so it rules out most South Africans. Perhaps a practising Christian who is able to love his neighbour in the true sense of the word; who has an idea of running a country; who is prepared to be kicked from all sides.

This situation led others to regard a foreigner as the most suitable:

> It must be someone from outside South Africa – Black or White – who has not learnt the advantages of being a White in South Africa otherwise he would perpetuate the system. The same applies to a Black person. I don't see anyone from South Africa managing to improve the situation.

The prospect of a foreigner was, however, unacceptable to others who again preferred to rely on a democratic system to produce the most appropriate person:

> In our situation it is difficult. Basic Black leadership has been snuffed out. We have figureheads like Mandela but we don't know what he would be like if he was out [of prison]. No one outside South Africa would fit in. It must be a local man. To try and find one man would be a recipe for disaster. Democracy must do it. We must get a person with leadership qualities who can get people together to find a compromise. Just a good leader who can build a good team in whom people of all shades can have confidence.

Given the problems such a leader would face, the qualities he/she required were considered messianic:

> A greathearted South African. A statesman rather than a politician who looks broader than ethnic association; who looks to the greater benefit of South Africa. A messiah. They are very scarce. There are some strong points and weaknesses in all the people I

can think of. It must be a man of great vision. It is a matter for the nation to come to after a very careful assessment of the strengths and weaknesses of various individuals. I would accept any person whose strengths are greater than his vices. It could be a White, Black, Coloured, or anyone, as long as it is a man of great vision.

This description of a charismatic type of a leader was also reflected by the names that were suggested as examples. The most often mentioned South African was the late Albert Luthuli, the African nationalist leader who was the first South African to receive the Nobel Peace Prize. He was followed by the imprisoned nationalist leader, Nelson Mandela. Other names mentioned were those of P. W. Botha, Chief Mangosuthu Buthelezi, Dr Gerrit Viljoen, the late General Jan Smuts, Gavin Relly, Dr Frederik Van Zyl Slabbert, the late Z. K. Matthews, Dr Sam Motsuenyane, Dr Anton Rupert, and Jan Steyn. A potentially unifying force that was often mentioned in connection with leadership was Christianity, as was illustrated with the motivation of Albert Luthuli as an example of an acceptable leader:

A practising Christian – anyone who wants to govern men and isn't that will not have any success. Albert Luthuli is an example of the man I'd like to see. Not only talking Christianity but doing it. Someone like that would bring more credibility to politics. Today, politics is something that is linked more to expediency than to principles. He must be colourblind. He mustn't be for any particular group. He must be for the people of the nation, someone who transcends limited sectional interests. That kind of leader we haven't been able to create. P. W. Botha does try, but he is a prisoner of what he believes is the overriding feeling of the *volk*, which a leader shouldn't be. I don't make anything of being a Tswana because I am a human being first.

Charismatic-type leaders also dominated the list of foreigners that were used as examples of suitable leaders: the late John F. Kennedy, the late Martin Luther King, Ronald Reagan, Robert Mugabe, Julius Nyerere, Jimmy Carter, the late Seretse Khama, and the late king Sobuza of Swaziland. This was expressed as follows:

We need someone who is educated, who is honest, who is loyal to South Africa. One that is not biased to any particular group, otherwise he would be un-South African. One that thinks anything that harms South Africa or causes unhappiness to anyone is un-South African. Someone who is keen on the development of the whole country, who cares for the poor, backward, aged, disabled. The ideal moves towards a Christ-follower. Among the human rulers I had respect for are John F. Kennedy and Albert Luthuli. The modern-day Nyerere.

Elites in Tanzania mentioned strength, humility, ability and correct political views as the most important leadership qualities required of a president, while the leaders they admired most were Julius Nyerere, John F. Kennedy and Kenneth Kaunda, in that order.[3]

Against this background of ideal leadership qualities described by the elite it is interesting to see how currently prominent South Africans were rated. Four men with a high public profile – the state president P. W. Botha, the imprisoned nationalist leader Nelson Mandela, the hereditary Zulu chief Mangosutho Buthelezi, and Anglican archbishop Desmond Tutu – were most often mentioned. The only unreserved judgement of worthiness to be the leader of a new South Africa was accorded Nelson Mandela. This was expressed as follows:

Previously I would have said Albert Luthuli. Now I think Nelson Mandela is our man. I knew him very well and keep contact with his wife. He was one of our greatest leaders. He is still up to the mark. He is mentally alert and still able to lead.

and:

Mandela. Refusing to take his freedom shows he is still active and OK. He is non-racial in everything. Contrary to what people think he is very non-violent. He has restrained more violence in the ANC second next to Luthuli. He has refused P. W. Botha's condition because he is in effect being asked to reject violence and then to step out into a violent situation.

Others that considered Mandela to be suitable as a type, rejected him as he was no longer active in society; for example:

It doesn't matter who he is as long as he is an able leader and has leadership qualities. Mandela is not ideal now. He is out of touch with realities. We need someone who is still relevant.

P. W. Botha was seen to be a possibility for the leadership of a new South Africa were he not bound by his constituency. This was expressed as follows:

A democrat to the bone. A fellow like P. W. Botha, given all the problems he must be facing within his party, is not a bad model. Not many leaders in South Africa would have done what he has dared. It is just too bad he has come in at a time when we want things higher than he can give.

Chief Buthelezi's leadership qualities were acknowledged while his emotionalism and sectional nationalism were rejected. For example:

Someone with vision and courage tempered with humaneness. And a firmness to take others seriously enough to involve them in decisions. With qualifications I'd suggest Buthelezi. He is too emotional but he does have vision and creativity.

and:

Buthelezi has made himself very unpopular because of his home-land affiliation and because of Inkatha, that tribal and exclusive Zulu movement of his. He is intelligent and does have the needs of the people at heart but he is very reactionary. If he is criticized in a newspaper he reacts sharply.

Desmond Tutu's religious work was admired but he was rejected as a politician:

I admire the courage of Tutu. He is my idol and he was my teacher but he doesn't have executive qualities.

and:

Nobody embodies the visions of society I'd like to see. If Albert Luthuli or Z. K. Matthews was still alive. They embodied some-thing beautiful – a deep spirit of tolerance. I see some of it in Desmond Tutu but he won't make a good politician.

Their description of a suitable political leader for a new South Africa as well as the qualities personified by the examples they offered, suggest that the elite consider a charismatic non-authoritarian type of personality best suited. Their orientations on this issue support indications in the discussion of African inclusion in the previous section that they identify with a broad South Africanism in which racial divisions are unimportant. Their rejection of an African as necessarily the only acceptable political leader for South Africa is a theme that is continued in their orientation to White fears.

WHITE FEARS

The political system in South Africa, while not a democratic one, is a power system based on representative government in which the leaders are elected by Whites who have a monopoly of power. For the system to be changed to a more democratic one in a non-revolutionary way, the Whites will have to agree to share power with Africans, since the numerical ratio between Whites and Africans is such that a non-discriminatory power-sharing system will turn the Whites into a minority group. It is widely argued that the reluctance of the Whites to agree to institute such changes derives from their fears of being swamped. These fears are real in the sense that they form part of their definition of the situation. It is therefore important to see whether the elite appreciates this dilemma and, if so, how they react to it.

All of the elite agreed that the fears Whites have of an African government was one of the main problems in achieving a democratic political system. White fears were interpreted in various ways although they were mostly seen as unfounded and a consequence of the political system. A typical remark was the following:

> If I was White I would be scared too, if I judge by the anger in the townships. If White leaders soften up, the Black people will relax. Blacks have a great capacity for forgiveness. This is the only place in the world where people joke about their situation instead of despairing. It is impossible to diminish White people's role in the community. We need them all. In Zimbabwe, Whites are returning. The holocaust that was predicted did not come. The problem will solve itself.

White fears were sometimes seen as a fear for their physical safety:

They have fear because if you have done bad on someone else there is a possibility of a backlash to do injustice on you. The more they delay the inevitable the more time they give Blacks to plan to do the same to Whites. Whites will not be eliminated. The sooner the change the less chance of a backlash. I don't hear talk of retribution for Whites. We must give each other a chance. There will be problems but a president must give everyone a chance. It is not a valid fear. We would vote for the best man. I'd like to have someone who will articulate my feelings irrespective of race. More Blacks would vote for Whites than Whites would vote for Blacks.

Most, however, interpreted White fears as fears for a loss of privilege:

Whites don't have reason to fear. I don't believe White fear is one of being outnumbered. They don't want to share power and privilege. It will affect their living standards. They don't want to let loose of what they have. We must have proportional representation and we must talk things over. Whites are very far from that.

A fear of being outnumbered was also recognised:

I'd exercise real justice to all population groups. The fears Whites have are that Blacks are the majority group who will kick Whites out of Parliament. That is not the case. We will still go for the best man. Look at what happened in Africa. We don't want dictatorships like that. If a government is not good at the next election we would chuck them out just like in Western-style governments.

Although they recognised White fears, many of the elite did not really understand them. For example:

For generations Whites have entrusted their children and households to Blacks as well as their most intimate personal needs. How can they be scared of a Black government?

White fears were perceived as unreasonable:

It is an unreasonable attitude of Whites that because they have been harsh and unkind to us they would expect us to do the same. I would be democratic without looking at colour.

White fears were also seen as an emotion that had been used to mobilize Whites to maintain their domination. For example:

Whites don't fear Blacks. They despise them. Because of their genetic or racial make-up Whites think they will outperform Blacks in anything they do. Whites fear they will lose the kind of jobs Blacks would do better. This fear psychosis is not real. I know very well that the homeland structures are built on ethnicity. We don't see Bantustans for English, Afrikaans, Italian or whatever – we just see White. They divide us so that we can be fighting ourselves. They had to separate people to perpetuate White domination. The Afrikaner group is determined to stay in power so they created differences to create Afrikanerness. It is a question of power. It is an imagined fear to promote political ambitions.

Most ascribed Whites' fears to fear of the unknown, in this case to a lack of knowledge about Africans brought about by the system of institutionalized racial separation. Their suggestions for allaying White fears stressed a solidarity of all South Africans, the principle of appointments based on merit and the necessity of creating unifying symbols. A common approach is exemplified by the following:

I'd tell them we are no different from each other; that the seeming diversity is a strength not a weakness; that the Blacks are not intrinsically evil people and unprincipled; that we are just as concerned as everyone else to live in peace and prosperity. I'd assure them a place in the sun and that the kind of hangups we have in South Africa are totally unnecessary; and that we are missing out on some of the joys we could be having out of life by bickering. I'd take people at their face value, accept them as honourable and committed to making a better life for all. Lots of laws in South Africa treat people as children and prevent them from doing certain things. I'd treat everyone as mature and responsible. An adult is an adult regardless of his colour. I'd scrap all this nonsense about separate areas and schools. They are totally unnecessary. People must choose who they want to associate with. This will prevent Blacks from taking revenge. We must forgive and forget. White fears are irrational. The fact that Blacks and Whites fought in the past – Shaka, Dingane and all the rest – doesn't mean that in the meantime we haven't been able to learn and to appreciate the qualities that each has got to bring in building a new nation of South Africans. I think we have tended to concentrate too much on the differences rather than concentrating on the strengths There will be differences in terms of people's views of life and lifestyle and things like that, but that doesn't make it to be a weakness. We see that happening in the United States – a nation which is made up of many smaller minority nationalities and it is a very cohesive nation. That doesn't mean they don't have problems They do. But they all have one allegiance, which is something that most South Africans don't feel, for example, what one sees in the South African flag. There is no affinity to that flag because it is something that you didn't take part in evolving.

A broad South African solidarity was seen to be achievable by bringing people together:

I would let them get to know each other as two different groups The fears are one-sided. Blacks know Whites but Whites don' know Black people. Most fears are of the unknown. The main cause of fear is ignorance. I'd bring Whites and Blacks together so that Whites can get to know Blacks better. In our building we share facilities. In the beginning it was strange but we got through all that to togetherness. Now it is normal. If the two groups got together more and more problems would be solved.

A solution in Whites becoming acquainted with the African lifestyle was also presented:

White South Africans should visit the townships. They just don' know how the other half lives. Mixed education will be a good investment for the future in the long run. The average Black child equates affluence with being White. It is the same on the other side. Whites think that struggling and being poor is what God ordained for Blacks. Contact will lead to less fear. Because of separation, mutual fears and suspicion are exacerbated both ways

Many respondents stressed the interdependence of all the people in the country. They felt that in a democratic system where merit was used as the main criterion for appointment, White fears would be allayed; for example:

The fear of White South Africans is a perceived fear. One would need to reassure white South Africa we are here together and need to work together. We are totally interdependent. We need to make the Whites feel at home. I would avoid appointments on the basis of colour and look at their abilities to bring into reality the interdependence we have in South Africa. A lot of Whites think one-man-one-vote means Black will vote for Black. The longer it takes to achieve one-man-one-vote the more likely that will be. People tend to look for the best man for the job. It would be wrong to kick Whites out of jobs and make them feel uncomfortable.

The theme of a South African solidarity in which Blacks would not necessarily vote for Blacks was taken up many times. It was pointed out that Whites had indispensable expertise, which was sometimes expressed very bluntly, as in: 'If the best man is Van der Merwe, we will vote for Van der Merwe.' There is, however, evidence in this that the elite do not fully understand the democratic process and the functioning of interest groups and the vote-capturing techniques that it implies, probably because of their own lack of exposure to it. The need to create unifying symbols was, however, recognised, and was expressed as follows:

I am very conscious of the need to help the nation build a transcending brotherhood. One of the great shortcomings of our age and society in South Africa is our preoccupation with colour consciousness. We have become so sectional it is an obsession. When I start thinking of the needs of my country I first think of my group's needs and interests and I relegate to the background the needs of other people. It is so unchristian to look at it this way. It is a great pity because we are a Christian country and Christian values are being sacrificed all the time. I believe the White people have lost their sense of mission. The other day I was reading into the history of the last century about Moshesh. Chief Moshesh heard of the noble deeds that the missionaries were doing in the Cape. They were freeing slaves, or speaking for the freedom of slaves, and one of the missionaries was Dr Phillip. And there was Dr Van der Kemp, and these fellows had come from overseas to preach to the Hottentots at places like Genadendal. Moshesh was so moved when he heard of the noble work of freeing the slaves that he sent 200 head of cattle down to the Cape to buy himself a missionary, a White one, who would come into Lesotho to bring about this message of reconciliation and freedom. Unfortunately

150 *The Modern African Elite of South Africa*

they didn't arrive at their destination but word did nevertheless reach the missionaries, who out of a deep sense of concern for the development of Christian work in Lesotho sent word to Paris and asked the Paris evangelical missionary group to establish themselves in the region, which they did in 1858. Now that history is forgotten. The times in our country when people had a deep sense of commitment to the freedom of people, of all people, irrespective of their colour, have been forgotten. I think we need to return to those times, especially the Whites. They have got the Christian mission. They have got all the other missions to open up, to become a little less possessive, less selfish. I can't see a government of the Black people that will totally exclude Whites from involvement. I would certainly allow the White people to become a part of my government. I don't think it would be realistic to visualize a government, a stable government, without the Whites, without the Coloureds, without all the other groups. We need a popular government which would be seen to be representing the interests of all groups in the country. Number two, you need competence. The competence of the people who are in administration that would put everyone's heart at ease that government is in the hands of the right people. Unless you have these two – representativeness and then competence – you are not going to run a successful government. The fear, I think, of the Whites to allow the Blacks to come in is based on preconceptions that are not justified.

A bill of rights is an example of a concrete solution suggested to create a common loyalty. For example:

I'm very conservative. My system would have a bill of rights to protect my minority rights but at the same time afford full freedom to people to pursue whatever goals they have in such a manner that their goals don't conflict with individual or group rights. We need the real American dream of freedom. One would have to find a system that protects the bill of rights. I'd do a lot of homework to avoid the Zimbabwe situation and avoid change after a new system has been accepted, like Mugabe did.

Another concrete suggestion was the appointment of Whites to certain portfolios. For example:

It is a real fear I can understand. What has happened in the rest of

Africa hasn't made the task easier for us. I'd immediately ensure a greater role for the White people, like in law and order, and leave it in the hands of Whites so that they can have a real interest and themselves protect their property and their rights.

While most of the elite recognised that White fears were real in their consequence and had suggestions for allaying them, a minority rejected any responsibility. For example:

I don't feel that I would be obliged to allay their fears. They must care for their own fears. They have been generated by Whites themselves by perpetuating the system. These fears began from an imaginary standpoint and are today a real issue.

THE FREE ENTERPRISE ECONOMIC SYSTEM

The free enterprise economic system is a recurring theme in the debate about new social structures for South Africa. Whites often express fears about the maintenance of the free enterprise system should Africans be included in central institutions. A perception exists that the fulfilment of African aspirations will damage the free enterprise system and even lead to communism.

The dominant economic system in South Africa is capitalism in which Africans are predominantly labourers. Although the elite are leaders in their occupations and have a wider experience of economic life than the rest of the African community, they display a lack of experience about free enterprise which they freely admitted. For example:

I don't know what the meaning of free enterprise is. If I were to say to you, yes, I like free enterprise, I would be fiddling in the dark because I just don't know what it is. Right now I am trying to get a site for a shopping centre on the East Rand but I continually find people saying, 'Hey, you don't belong there.'

The elite nevertheless felt comfortable with the concept of free enterprise, and all but four of them supported it. The other four preferred some form of mixed economic system with free entrepreneurship and centralized social services. Although, because of the government's attitude to communism and legal measures to suppress it, one would not expect anyone to express explicit support for communism, the elite were quite obviously not a majority of marxists. The Buthelezi Commission had a similar finding, namely that Africans in general displayed no systematic hostility for private enterprise.[4] Because of their status the elite see the benefits that Whites derive from free enterprise. Young people without similar exposure could be expected to favour other economic systems, which probably explains the attitudes reported of youth leaders. On the other hand, it has repeatedly been found around the world that upward mobility results in political conservatism, i.e. support for the prevailing ideology.[5]

There was a clear pattern of support for the free enterprise system although they were unanimous in their opinion that the African community was excluded from participation in it. This was expressed as follows:

> I believe in free enterprise not because it is an affair of the White man, not because it is an affair of the fat cats who are getting something out of the backs of those that are downtrodden, but because it agrees with my basic Christian philosophy of the right and responsibility of the individual to make a contribution and be accountable. I'm not saying what we see in South Africa is the genuine article. It is not. What we see in South Africa is in fact a system predicated on a certain section benefiting at the expense of the other. We do see some products of free enterprise in some areas of the country, but basically it is not. When the government talks about free enterprise they don't understand what they are talking about. They are saying something they are totally negating by their actions and their policies. The result is that in the processs the Black people, not being able to separate the wheat, see the chaff as the genuine product and they reject it, and rightly so, because we cannot have apartheid and free enterprise. The Black people equate free enterprise with apartheid and oppression and all the negative things.

The possibility of the African community supporting communism because of their lack of experience of the benefits of the free enterprise system, was often expressed. For example:

> Unless greater emphasis is placed on free enterprise we are playing into the hands of the communists. What is there for Blacks in free

enterprise? We have not seen any benefits in free enterprise. We have not been shown anything bad in socialism.

Although the families of the elite enjoyed a higher socio-economic status than the rest of the African community, there was also evidence of support for communism among them. This was illustrated by the concern of a father:

My fears are that the Black population will gradually turn communist. My son says he is a communist but I know nothing good will come out of it. More and more are driven to it. It has proved a disaster in Africa.

Because of the negative evaluation of free enterprise in the African community, businessmen found that they were regarded with suspicion; for example:

The competitive spirit sparks you to be creative. It is an incentive and it results in efficiency. We as Blacks have always had this feeling. We had a lot of cattle but also a lot of sharing. It looks like a feudal system but it has a thread of free enterprise. Free enterprise is a good system. It is unfortunate that in South Africa it is not practised. I can't open my factory where I want to. I am far from my market which is the metropolitan area. My factory should be there. The denial of opportunities to Blacks makes them look outside free enterprise. My fear is that they will aspire to socialism. They are not allowed to taste the free enterprise system in South Africa. They think Blacks succeed because they are given preference of some sort by the government. So successful people are seen as stooges and young people opt for socialism. They say it is not possible for a Black person to succeed in this country.

The manifestation of South African capitalism as advantageous to the White community while the African community maintains a low standard of living, is the main motivation for the minority feeling that South Africa would best be served by a mixed economic system. This is not a rejection of the free enterprise system as such but rather a reaction to the result of African exclusion from it. The desirability of a mixed economic system was motivated as follows:

Free enterprise has certain limitations as it tends to favour the powerful. Whites gain by free enterprise while the Blacks are very negative about it. The political context has to change before we can even talk about free enterprise. To enthuse Blacks about the system you must talk on a political level. I'd be open to a mixed economic system by taking the best of socialism and the best of free enterprise. Some aspects of the economy must be state controlled, for example schools, security forces, hospitals. But transport should be privatized. It brings competition and involvement and creates dynamism. We should learn from the German economy and their social-democratic system.

The Afrikaners' management of the economy after they came to power in 1948 was seen as a model for African advancement; for example:

I would strive for a mixed economy because of the backlog among Blacks. The same as in 1948 when the Afrikaners adapted free enterprise to catch up on the Afrikaner backlog. We must set up processes to get a better filtering of wealth. We need a type of socialist state to close up the gap while the people can retain initiative. Every individual must work as hard as possible in life but wealth cannot be left in the hands of a few. Land not effectively used must be made available to others to build houses on and develop.

There was also disparagement about the way the Afrikaners had controlled the economy; for example:

I find this very interesting. At the turn of the century Afrikaner politicians regarded themselves as socialist and anti-capitalist. This led to the strikes of 1922. Later they formed big corporations like the parastatals to promote Afrikaner interests. Now that the Afrikaner has arrived and they use taxpayers' money to promote their own interests they talk of free enterprise. As far as Blacks are concerned South Africa is terribly regulated. There is absolutely no evidence of free enterprise for Blacks.

Naked capitalism did, however, not hold favour:

The *laissez-faire* kind of capitalism of the United States at the turn of the century I wouldn't like to see visited on my people either.

Today, big business has developed a social conscience which is an improvement. I like free enterprise with a social conscience providing housing, education and transport. The profit motive mustn't be the only motive.

The elite's appraisal of the free enterprise economic system was based on its manifestation in South African society. They nevertheless considered it the most appropriate system but insisted that Africans be included in it.

CONCLUSION

The socio-political orientations of the elite reflect the political reality of the African community, namely their exclusion from central political structures. They reject the ideology of group differentiation and prefer a system that does not reflect racial and ethnic divisions because of the African community's bad experience of the present system. In their orientations to the potential leadership of a new South Africa and White fears of Black domination, they display a non-revengeful ideal of a broad South African solidarity similar to the so-called American dream in which everyone has the same opportunities. Likewise they support the free enterprise economic system because of the benefits the White community has been seen to derive from it and want to be included in it. They can, therefore, not be regarded as political radicals. They merely want to be meaningfully included in the Western-type societal system that the White community has established in South Africa on an equal basis with Whites, as they have already adopted most of the White community's Western-orientated values.

7 Conclusion

Studies of elites (also called opinion-leaders) have been undertaken in societies and communities around the world, illuminating the processes involved in social power. Different definitions of the term 'elite' have been used for different studies while not all studies have concentrated on the same processes. The common feature of these studies, namely a concern with a category of people at the top of status hierarchies, was the starting-point for this study which presents a profile of the modern African elite of South Africa.

Elites exist in all societies. In undifferentiated, pre-modern societies elite status is mostly based on hereditary succession and the management of all spheres of activity resides in the same people. For example, in traditional African society the hereditary chief and his headmen take all the decisions relating to the tribe, whether of a religious, economic, political or whatever nature. With modernization, societies differentiate functionally and these roles (religious, economic, etc.) are assumed by different people on the basis of their individual proficiency. Separate institutional complexes each with its own status hierarchy develop around these roles. A variety of people then occupy high-status positions collectively forming the modern social elite. The status of modern elites is therefore based on achievement in contrast to the ascribed status of traditional elites.

The working definition used in this study views the modern African elite as the incumbents of functionally important positions in various institutional complexes in the modern African community. It therefore deals with the elites that have gained their status through achievement, and excludes traditional elites. The complexes that were included are those that are most prominent in the modern African community, namely the business sector, religion, professions and community life. The polity had to be excluded, as the modern African community outside the national and independent states in South Africa is not included in the institutionalized political structure at central government level.

The positional and reputational approaches were used to identify the appropriate individuals at the top of the four institutional complexes mentioned above. In the business sector, three subsectors were distinguished, namely entrepreneurs, trade unionists and managers in white-controlled companies. Five opinion-leaders from each of these sectors were interviewed. In the professional sector, leaders from medicine, law, nursing, social work, education and journalism were included, and in the religious sector the leaders of the most prominent churches in the African community. Five leaders each from sports administration, art and women's activities were interviewed as representatives of community life. Only three of the sixty people originally identified for inclusion refused or were unavailable. The interviews took place all over South Africa from May to August 1985 on the basis of an interview guide. All the people interviewed are well known in the modern African community and are prominent names in their national occupational spheres.

The relationship between the various race groups and communities in South Africa and consequently the development and social role of the modern African elite, are a result of the socio-political history of South Africa, which differs significantly from that of Black Africa. The reality of the economic 'decay' of many societies in Africa is accepted by economic historians and has been attributed to superficial capitalism, since, *inter alia*, contact with the colonial powers was too brief to have a lasting impact on societal development, Western consumption patterns were adopted more effectively than Western production techniques, urbanization occurred without industrialization, and societies that were stateless in pre-colonial times had to become states within one generation – with the result that Westernization took place without modernization.[1] However, none of this applies to South Africa. The development of South Africa has taken a different course from that of the rest of Africa, especially in regard to the time dimension. Modern Westernization based on extensive industrialization started in South Africa many generations ago, while Africans began to internalize Western values from their contact with White settlers even earlier. As industrialization spread, a comprehensive social structure with a capitalist economic system developed and increasing numbers of Africans were incorporated into it from their traditional subsistence economy. For a long time they participated in the industrial sector as low-paid labourers, as this was all that the social system allowed them. As their incorporation into the modern socio-economic system gained momentum, they discarded more and more elements of their traditional lifestyle and adopted Western culture patterns from the Whites for whom they worked. The fact that the White-controlled government adopted measures to prevent their full incorporation into the modern economy and tried to confine them to the traditional sector and lower-level job-opportunities in the industrial sector, did not stop this process but led to widespread frustration in the African community as it interfered with this process of social development. The relative poverty of the African community in spite of its incorporation into the modern economy, is therefore more the result of its low social status and the unequal distribution of resources caused by statutory racial discrimination than the consequence of its racial heritage. As time went by, Africans progressed into higher-level occupations although they never enjoyed the same opportunities as did Whites. They did not have the same educational opportunities, while there were various other socio-political constraints on their upward mobility. Initially their occupational advance was limited to the occupations associated with serving their own community, such as religion and education. Over time, as the economy diversified and manpower needs expanded, they also began to enter other occupational fields including business and the professions in which they advanced, with those reaching the top forming the category of people known as social elites. Africans are gradually also being included in the general South African elites. Even though traditional rural settlements similar to those of the subsistence economic system persisted (and can still be found), people living in them became increasingly dependent on the urban economy, and today few can survive without the financial contributions of urban relatives and pensions from the central government. The Westernization of the African community of South Africa is therefore more widespread and deep-seated than that of most other societies in Africa, and a scenario for South Africa of economic collapse under African government such as has occurred in many other parts of Africa is not realistic. Africans in South Africa are, however, as yet still excluded from the institutionalized political system of the broader South African society, and consequently no legitimate political elite can be identified in the African community. Africans are therefore not yet included fully in the societal community of South Africa, although current developments in the country are primarily concerned with this issue.

The information obtained in the interviews with the elite shows that the leadership category in the African community has become as Westernized as the White population. Their characteristics follow the same pattern as those elites in other Western societies. African elites are largely male and over the age of fifty, as in the case in other modern societies where leadership roles are the result of individual achievement. They were socialized in conjugal families that were highly placed in the African stratification system of their time, and had internalized the Western social value system which included achievement-orientated values. Their parents and grandfathers were better educated and practised higher occupations than the rest of the African community of their time, although they were still far behind the average for the White community. There is a strong urban bias among the elite. Most of them live in a metropolitan area while many of them grew up there. Their urbanism and the tendency of their forefathers to move to the urban areas follows the general pattern of African urbanization which accompanied the industrialization of South Africa.

The elite were more fortunate than the rest of the African population in their educational opportunities. They were socialized in homes where their grandfathers and parents were better educated than the rest of the African community of their time and had emphasized the value of education. Probably because they did well at school other relatives and teachers helped with the elite's education when their own parents were unable to do so. On their part, the elite used all the opportunities they could get to advance themselves educationally. More than four-fifths of them eventually attained tertiary qualifications while almost a third hold advanced degrees. During their socialization they internalized Western achievement-oriented values and their career histories show that they advanced rapidly to formal leadership roles where they externalize Western values. Most of them started their careers in professional posts after full-time training, while a minority took any job they could get and studied in their spare time. They tended to stay in the profession for which they were originally trained.

Most of them work in private sector organizations mainly under African control. In this connection it should be noted that until fairly recently constraints on the upward mobility of Africans operated in most White-controlled organizations. In many instances the elite are self-employed or are themselves employers. Most of them work in the highly industrialized area of the Witwatersrand where most of the advanced occupational opportunities occur. Their incomes compare well with the average for Whites in comparable occupations although they probably earn less than the White elite.

Besides overcoming constraints imposed by the general poverty level in the African community to become educated and advance to a high occupational status, the elite also had to overcome legal constraints on the mobility of Africans imposed by the political system, such as influx control. In addition they were targets of the security system which functions to obviate resistance to the prevailing political system. They attracted the attention of the security agents because of their visible upward mobility and social prominence. Most of them mentioned unpleasant experiences which even led some of them to refuse to co-operate with any government-linked organization on any matter at all. Because the security system is seen to serve the interests of the White community, it can be expected that these activities of security agencies would be an important factor alienating the elite in the African community from the government and making them unwilling to co-operate with the government in the quest for a solution to the country's political problem.

In their own assessment of their achievements the elite ascribed their upward mobility to personal characteristics such as self-motivation, courage, flexibility, leadership qualities and a passion for challenges. This reflects the motivational factors encompassed by their need to achieve which they had internalized as part of the Western value system. The drive to achieve is a well-known middle-class phenomenon in Western societies.

Their family life follows the pattern found in other modern Western societies. They selected marriage partners with a similar background to their own, who came from the highly educated sector of their community, while the men were better educated than their wives. There was no clear male dominance and decision-making and role divisions suggest a trend towards egalitarian marital relationships. Their families were still relatively large when compared with White families but very much smaller than those they grew up in, which is a well-known pattern in modernizing societies. The elite had a clear preference for professional occupational training for their children and encouraged them to study, thereby repeating their own socialization by inculcating Western achievement values in their children. The majority of their children were involved in, or had completed, university training.

There are indications of a strong religious tendency among the elite. They regularly attended services in formally organized churches. This provides evidence in support of a trend of conventionality in terms of the urban middle-class value system of modern Western-type societies that emerges throughout the study.

The elite used their leisure time for activities common to Westernized societies, although they preferred quieter activities than the rest of the population, probably because of their busy and stimulating

work schedule. Their reading and music tastes were very sophisticated as, for example, most of them enjoyed listening to classical
music. Although the lifestyle of the elite is more sophisticated, it is
not unusual in the African community: market research surveys have
shown that Africans generally have the same consumption patterns
and preferences as whites. The elites played a leading role in a variety
of informal organizations that serve their community, indicating that
their leadership is accepted by the general African community and
that they are accepted as role models. Their extensive travel to other
parts of the world, mainly in connection with their work, brought
them into contact with international leaders in their respective fields.
This also means that leaders in other societies were exposed to them
and can in turn be expected to judge the potentialities of Africans in
South Africa as well as their capabilities for playing a meaningful
political role in terms of Western values from their evaluation of the
elite.

Despite the accentuation of ethnicity in the socio-political structures of South Africa, the elite attached very little relevance to their
tribal ethnic extraction. They intensely disliked the importance attached to it officially which they saw as a political instrument aimed at
dividing the African community, and were disparaging of attempts by
African leaders to mobilize ethnicity for political purposes. Their
ethnic attachments were very weak and those that still exist can be
explained by geographic factors and the consequent kinship links.
The conservatism that they display as part of their middle-class
lifestyle is therefore more firmly rooted in the Westernized sector of
South African society than in the traditional sector. There is no
evidence of an ethnic nationalism in any other terms than that of
being African in a multiracial South Africa. This will probably eventually disappear into a broad South African nationalism as the criterion
of race for the ordering of society recedes in importance. Their
rejection of the importance that the government places on ethnicity
in the ordering of society is shared by the general African population,
and was indicated by the research referred to in Chapter 5.

There is strong evidence that other characteristics such as educational level are more important than ethnicity in the selection of
spouses, which is usually regarded as a good indicator of group
consciousness. There is a divergence of opinion on the customs of
lobola and ancestor veneration, with the arguments for and against
these practices being based on their functionality in the modern
environment. The protagonists of lobola, for example, cite the high

incidence of divorce in modern society and see lobola as a means of making marriage formation difficult and involving both families in the union. These customs have been adapted to the modern environment, and the fact that those that practise one of them do not necessarily practise the other, strengthens the evidence that traditional customs have come to be judged on the grounds of their functionality and are not the manifestation of a blind adherence to custom. The fact that the elite, together with other groups in the African community, might participate in traditional customs therefore does not disqualify them from the label 'Westernized', just as it does not disqualify other tradition-rich groups in South Africa. In the case of Africans, apparent traditionality is largely a function of a lifestyle under conditions of poverty. There is in any case no evidence that their traditional heritage causes the elite any discomfort in their modern environment.

The socio-political views of the elite also reflect a strong orientation towards Western-type values in spite of their exclusion from the institutionalized political process in the modern sector of South African society. They all recognize African exclusion as the crucial problem facing South Africa. The solution they present is the inclusion of Africans in the democratic political process either in a unitary state or in a federal system. None of the elite unconditionally thought that a socio-political system acceptable to Africans could incrementally be evolved out of the present system. The majority felt that a national meeting of legitimate leaders would have to devise a completely new system, while a minority felt that if legitimate African leaders were involved, all formal racial differentiation were abandoned and the government convinced Africans that it was serious about reform by acting as fast as possible, a system acceptable to everyone could be evolved out of the existing one.

The qualities the elite considered a prerequisite for the leader of a new South Africa again illustrates their preference for Western democratic values. More than half of them regarded a non-racial and non-ethnic disposition to be the most important quality required of a leader. The examples of leadership types they cited reflected a preference for charismatic, non-authoritarian personalities. Their evaluation of suitable leaders presents evidence that they form their own opinions, and are not influenced by controversies surrounding particular personalities or government attempts to discredit supposed leaders who are critical of the government. Their long-standing mistrust of the government's policies and strategies would also play a role in their evaluation of current events.

The elite regarded the fears that Whites have of an African government as the main problem in achieving a democratic political system. They nevertheless felt that this fear is irrational and would prove unfounded in a truly democratic system. Suggestions such as assisting the different races to get to know one another better by means of greater contact, assigning government functions such as the maintenance of law and order to Whites, and a bill of individual rights, were offered as ways of allaying the fears of Whites.

The elite supports the basic premises of the free enterprise economic system (although not naked capitalism) and wishes that their community could be included in it. They were concerned that the prevailing political system is driving part of the African community, notably the youth, to communism.

In short, the results indicate that the elite have become successfully Westernized. The relevance of their strong Western orientation lies in the fact that elites in other societies have been found to be trend-setters and to reflect dominant social values. The extent of the elite's advance into the upper echelons of the modern Western economic system in South Africa is still unusual for their community, as the societal constraints on the upward mobility of Africans are still so strong that relatively few have as yet been able to transcend them. However, as the modern industrial system is firmly established in South Africa and most Africans are already incorporated into it, albeit largely still on a low social level, the strong pressures on society to open up, including the movement towards universal Western-type education for Africans, can be expected to result in the rest of the African community also rapidly advancing to an economically more dominant role. The elite has already established education as the key vehicle for upward mobility, and the enormous demand for education and even its politicization suggests that education will also be the main means of advancement for the broader African community. The strong leadership role that the elites play at a lower social level in their community, indicating that they are accepted as role models in their community as was discussed in Chapter 4, suggests that their lifestyle will also be the one the broader African population will follow. This also means that the African population will have to be formally incorporated into the modern sector of society and accepted into the dominant societal community. If the total disruption of

South African society is to be avoided, the institutionalized normative culture that was structured to serve the interests of Whites, and in particular that of Afrikaner nationalism, will now have to be restructured to serve a broader South African nationalism which encompasses African nationalism. The evidence from the modern African elite suggests that this can be accomplished within the framework of Western-type social structures.

Besides being a ruling class, the elites of other societies have been found to be cohesive and ideologically unified. Because of the state of social evolution in South Africa, the African elite can as yet only be described as a potential part of the ruling class. It has achieved this status as a result of its socialization in terms of Western achievement-orientated values and its use of education as a mechanism for upward mobility. The fact that the African elite is still small and plays a minor role in the ordering of society, can be attributed to the constraints on the upward mobility of Africans operative in South Africa and the fact that relatively few Africans have as yet been able to transcend them. For the elite to constitute a cohesive or integrated category would imply a Weberian-type class formation in the African community. This has not happened in other parts of Africa largely because of the extended family system which retains close links between people of disparate social levels. In the African community of South Africa the full dynamics of stratification do not function because of constraints imposed by the political system, and consequently class formation cannot be determined. The class consciousness that is evident can be explained in terms of Marxist class distinctions, and is again the result of the political system. The African elites are, however, currently unified ideologically if their socio-political orientations are used as criteria. They consistently oppose the prevailing political system although they support the free enterprise system and the basic premises of Western democracy.

Apart from being fraught with methodological disputes, elite studies generate virulent theoretical debates because of the role of ideology in the social sciences. The choice of elitism as theme is in itself controversial, as elites have generally been found to be supportive of the status quo and to reflect conservative societal values. This study has hopefully shown the value of elite studies in describing the processes involved in leadership formation, even when the elite, though they might be conservative in many aspects of their lifestyle, do not support the status quo, in this case the political structuring of South Africa.

Although elite theory is often used as an approach in the study of people in positions of leadership, it has still not been successfully developed in the social sciences. Political scientists have used the elite hypothesis to identify people in positions of political power without explaining the social processes involved. Elite theory is not prominent in the mainstream of sociological thought, although studies such as this one of the African social elite have shown its value even if only in the conceptualization of a clearly apparent empirical phenomenon, namely the existence of a category of people at the top of social hierarchies. That elites similar to the elites of other societies exist in the urbanized African community of South Africa has also been shown by this study. It emerged from the preceding chapters that there are more similarities than differences between the development and characteristics of the African elite of South Africa and the elites of other Westernized societies. An interesting point is that this is true even though the political elite in the African community was excluded. There is in any case no reason to believe that the people who would emerge as political elite in an open South Africa would be any different from the social elites that were analysed. In other societies the difference between political elites and other elites has merely been one of occupational choice, with people moving to and fro between elite categories. Representatives of the urbanized African elite of this study also indicated that they are amenable to becoming involved in politics in a new South Africa. This means that just as the social elites that have emerged over generations in a variety of spheres in the urbanized African community are fully Westernized, the same can be expected of a political elite that would emerge in an open South Africa. That it proved too difficult to identify a political elite in the modern sector of the African community is therefore not the fault of elite methodology. It is the abnormality of South African society, with its system of institutionalized racial discrimination and rigid controls devised to maintain White domination, that has precluded the development of a Western-type African political elite.

Coming back to the empirical results of this study, there are nevertheless dangers in inferring too much about the political values of the African community from the orientations of the elite, as a community's power values are usually externalized by its institutionalized political elite and none exists as yet for the African community in White-controlled South Africa. As second best, African social elites may externalize prevalent values, but as beneficiaries to some extent of the modern achievement system they can be expected to support its basic premises even though they do not participate fully. The orientations of the elite therefore suggest that the more Africans perceive themselves to benefit from the achievement system of modern society, the more they are likely to support the normative premises underlying it. On the other hand, the elite's high level of identification with problems on a lower social level, as reflected by their involvement in voluntary work in their community, coupled with their acceptance of organizations such as the United Democratic Front and African National Congress and their leaders – in spite of government attempts at driving a wedge between these organizations and the rest of the African community and at labelling Africans amenable to government strategies as legitimate leaders – suggest that there is an ideological solidarity among Africans in the modern sector which the elite would reflect. Nevertheless, the only legitimate way of determining the political values of a community lies in the democratic political process. The results of this study suggest that the White community in South Africa need not be afraid of incorporating the Africans into the democratic political process, since those that emerge as social leaders generally subscribe to a Western-type value system.

Appendix: Interview Guide

A. BACKGROUND DETAILS

1. Sex.
2. Age (20–29, 30–39, 40–49, 50–59, 60–69, 70+).
3. Sector (economy, religion, professions, arts, feminists, sport).
4. Geographic location of work place.
5. Present position.
6. Number of years spent in present position.
7. Present income before deductions (up to R14 999, R15 000–19 999, R20 000–24 999, R25 000–29 999, R30 000–34 999, R35 000–39 999, R40 000–44 999, R45 000–49 999, R50 000–54 999, R55 000+)
8. How many people work under you? (Blacks/Whites/others?)

B. EDUCATION

9. Where did you mainly go to school? Name the place.
10. What kind of school was it?
11. In what area did you mainly live while you were growing up?
12. At what standard did you leave formal school?
13. What training did you receive after that?
14. Do you have any other qualifications?
15. Were your immediate post-school studies part-time or full-time?

C. CAREER

16. Describe your first job.
17. How did your career progress after that?
18. At what stage did you obtain permanent urban rights?

D. FUTURE

19. What is the ultimate position you would like to attain in your career?
20. If you could start your career and education over again, what would you do?

E. SELF APPRAISAL

21. You have beaten the system and made it to the top. How come? To what do you ascribe your particular success? Breakthroughs?

F. INFLUENCES

22. Did anyone have a particular influence on you while you were growing up or during your early career that steered your life in a certain direction? Discuss.

G. FAMILY

23. Are you married? If so, how were you married to your present wife/husband?
24. What educational level has your wife/husband attained?
25. What work does your wife/husband do at present.
26. What work did he/she do at the time that you were married?
    Now I'd like to speak about your parents.
27. Where did your mother mainly live while you were growing up?
28. Did your father live with you while you were growing up? If he did not, were was he?
29. If you did not live with your mother while you were growing up, with whom did you live and why?
30. What education did your father have?
31. What work did your father do?
32. What education did your mother have?
33. What work did your mother do?
34. What education did your father's father have?
35. What work did your father's father do?
36. Where did your father's father mainly live during his lifetime?
37. How were your parents married?

H. SIBLINGS AND OWN CHILDREN

38. How many brothers and sisters did you have?
39. Where did you fit in in the family structure?
40. Would you say that your brothers and sisters have attained the same level of achievement as you have, or is your achievement level higher or lower than theirs?
41. How many children do you have? Sons/daughters?
42. What kind of career would you like your sons and daughters to follow or

would you have liked them to follow? What are they doing now?
43. Do you expect lobola for your daughters or would you expect it if you had daughters? Explain.
44. How would you prefer your children to be married?

I. FAMILY LIFE

45. Who generally makes the big decisions in your home, e.g. to buy new furniture, build a room on to the house or have another child? Husband/ wife/both together?
46. Please tell me how you divide duties at home. What duties does the wife attend to and what does the husband attend to? Do you have domestic help?
47. What church do you attend?
48. How often do you attend religious services?
49. Do you honour the spirits of your ancestors? If so, in what way?

J. AFFILIATIONS

50. Of which voluntary organizations are you an active member?
51. Which ethnic group do you belong to?
52. Which ethnic group does your wife/husband belong to?
53. What exactly does your ethnic extraction mean to you?

K. LIFESTYLE

54. What do you like doing most when you relax?
55. What kind of books do you most like reading?
56. What newspapers do you read?
57. What kind of music do you like most?
58. Do you take an active part in sport? As a spectator?
59. How do you spend your holidays?
60. What experience do you have of travel outside South Africa?
61. What bugs you most about life?

L. ATTITUDES

62. If you think of someone who could govern a new South Africa in which everyone's political aspirations are met, what kind of person would that be? What qualities would that person have? Can you think of an example of that kind of person?

63. If you became the president of South Africa, how would you allay the fears Whites have of Black leadership?
64. Do you think it is possible to achieve a social system which is agreeable to Blacks by working within present structures? If so how should the process be set in motion?
65. Much has been said about maintaining a free enterprise economic system in South Africa. What are your views on this?
66. What would you say are the greatest problems facing South Africa today? Do you have suggestions for tackling these problems?
67. What would you say are the two greatest problems within your field of activity? Do you have suggestions for tackling them?
68. Have you ever been bothered by the security police? Explain.

Notes and References

1 Introduction

1. This section is based on the Human Sciences Research Council's report, *The South African Society: Realities and Future Prospects*, 1985.
2. Examples are Ayandele (1974) in Nigeria, Baltzell (1966) in America, Barton *et al.* (1973) in Yugoslavia, Brandel-Syrier (1971) in South Africa, Frey (1965) in Turkey, Guttsman (1963) in Britain, Higley *et al.* (1976 and 1979) in Norway and Australia, Hunter (1963) in America, Lloyd (1966) in tropical Africa, Suleiman (1978) in France, Van der Merwe (1974) in South Africa and Zartman (1980) in the Middle East.
3. See *The Power Elite*, 1956.
4. See *Community Power Structure*, 1953.
5. See *Who Governs?*, 1961.
6. See Bottomore (1976), Giddens (1972), Parry (1969), Field and Higley (1980).

2 Origin and Early Socialization

1. Dye and Pickering (1974).
2. See Van der Merwe *et al.* (1974:27) in respect of South Africa, Higley *et al.* (1976:169) in respect of Norway, and Higley, Deacon and Smart (1979:65) for Australia.
3. Because of the ambiguity in the use of the term 'elite' in different studies, the comparisons with other societies do not necessarily refer to exactly the same category of people. They are nevertheless presented as a broad contextualization.
4. For example, America (Dye and Pickering, 1974), Brazil (Manwaring, 1978) and Norway (Higley *et al.*, 1976:169). Among White South Africans (Van der Merwe *et al.*, 1974:25), West Germans (Roberts, 1972:145) and Australians (Higley, Deacon and Smart, 1979:65) the elite were found to be in their fifties, while the average age of elites in Tanzania (Hopkins, 1971: 74) was 39.
5. Cf. Smit en Kok (1981:19).
6. Statistics for the total African (and White) population of the RSA are offered here and elsewhere as a comparison to demonstrate the magnitude of the difference between the elite and the general population, although the statistical base is not always strictly comparable as Transkei, Bophuthatswana, Ciskei and Venda are usually excluded due to the lack of statistics.
7. Cf. Smit and Booysen (1981:44).
8. For example, America (Dye and Pickering, 1974), Turkey (Frey, 1965:133), Mexico (Smith, 1979) and Africa as a whole (Abu-Lughod,

1967:47). In South Africa, Afrikaans elites were found to have a predominantly rural background, while English-speaking elites had an urban background (Van der Merwe *et al.*, 1974:41). In Tanzania (Hopkins, 1971:74) and in five of seven societies in the Middle East (Tachau, 1975:297–8), elites were found to be of the first generation to move from a traditional, rural environment. This comparative data seems to suggest that elites in newly developing societies have a stronger rural background than those in already modernized societies.

9. See *Senate Debates*, 7 June 1954, columns 2599 and 2606.
10. Ministerial press release.
11. See Dye and Pickering (1974) in respect of America; Hopkins (1971:75) in respect of Tanzania; and Van der Merwe *et al.* (1974:54) in respect of South Africa.
12. Source: RSA Department of Education and Training.
13. See Lloyd (1966:28).
14. See Van der Merwe *et al.* (1974:84).
15. See Higley, Deacon and Smart (1979:82).
16. Cf. Peil (1982:207).
17. Cf. Peil (1982:85–9, 205–11).
18. For example, the Philippines (Abueva, 1968:278), Brazil (Manwaring, 1978, and DcDonough, 1981:58), Mexico (Smith, 1979:78), Ghana (Jahoda, 1966), Australia (Higley, Deacon and Smart, 1979:79–82), West Germany (Roberts, 1972:145), America (Mills, 1979:279), Egypt (Dekmejian, 1971:187), White South Africa (Van der Merwe *et al.*, 1972:82), Norway (Higley *et al.*, 1979:179), the Middle East (Tachau, 1975:60), Turkey (Frey, 1965:139–40) and East Africa (Goldthorpe, 1955).
19. See Wallerstein (1965).
20. See Hopkins (1971:70).
21. Cf. Sewell and Shah (1967), Rosen (1956) and Reissman (1953).
22. See Charton (1976).
23. For example, Brazil (Manwaring, 1978), America (Dye and Pickering, 1974), Nigeria (Plotnicov, 1970:278), Iran, Iraq and Israel (Lenczowski, 1975:27, 113, 186), the Belgian Congo (Brausch, 1956), West Africa (Wallerstein, 1965), Senegal (Mercier, 1965), the Middle East (Zartman, 1980:5), Latin America (Lipset and Solari, 1967:25), Australia (Higley, Deacon and Smart, 1979:84–5) and Mexico (Smith, 1979:82). Eighty per cent of White South African elites were found to have post-school qualifications, and 65 per cent of them degrees. Fifteen per cent held doctorates (Van der Merwe *et al.*, 1974:25, 58, 84).
24. Certain categories of professionals could get exemption from influx control regulations in terms of the Bantu (Urban Areas) Consolidation Act (No. 25 of 1954). Influx control in that form was abandoned during 1986.
25. See McClelland (1963:86, 92).
26. Cf. Prekel (1986) and Epstein (1973).
27. See McClelland (1963:86).

3 Career

1. For example, Saudi Arabia (Wenner, 1975:177) and Syria (Van Dusen, 1975:140).
2. Africa: for example, Hopkins (1971:74) in respect of Tanzania, and Lloyd (1966) of Tropical Africa; Latin America: for example, Smith (1979:199), Lipset and Solari (1967) and DcDonough (1981:73); Western societies: for example, Porter (1965) in respect of Canada, Higley *et al.* (1976) in respect of Norway, Mills (1979:279) in respect of the United States, Higley, Deacon and Smart (1979:84) in respect of Australia, and Van der Merwe *et al.* (1974:84) in respect of White South Africa; and the Middle East: for example, Abdel-Malek (1968:174) and Dekmejian (1971:184) in respect of Egypt, Zonis (1975:200) in respect of Iran, and Frey (1965:50) in respect of Turkey; as well as Russia: for example, Stewart (1968:142).
3. See Vallier (1967).
4. Zartman (1980:3).
5. See Beteille (1967).
6. Brandel-Syrier (1978:146–7).
7. See Van der Merwe *et al.* (1974:24–5), Abu-Lughod (1967:47), Ratinoff (1967) and Mills (1979:279).
8. See Van der Merwe *et al.* (1974:85), Mills (1979:9), Higley, Deacon and Smart (1979:65), Lukhero (1966), Plotnicov (1970:278), Goldthorpe (1955), Wallerstein (1965), Hopkins (1971:70), Manwaring (1978) and Bottomore (1967).
9. See Goldthorpe (1984:96).
10. Cf. Cilliers (1986a).
11. See Giliomee and Schlemmer (1985:1).
12. See RSA, President's Council (1985:148).
13. See Cilliers (1986b).
14. See South African Institute of Race Relations (1985:757–802).
15. See Market Research Africa (1986).

4 Lifestyle

1. See Goldthorpe (1955).
2. See Van der Walt (1977:43) and Mokoatle (1978:224).
3. See Higley, Deacon and Smart (1979:82–3) and Mills (1979:281).
4. See Moller (part 5, 1972:67–74).
5. See Lloyd (1966:30) and Hopkins (1971:71).
6. See Motshologane (1978). This is confirmed by Strijdom and Van der Burgh (1980:18).
7. See Coertze (1972a).
8. Cf. Motshologane (1978) and Strijdom and Van der Burgh (1980:10).
9. See Kies (1982:16).
10. See RSA, President's Council (1983:47).
11. See Goldthorpe (1955).
12. See Mercier (1956).

174 *Notes and References*

13. See Vorster (1970).
14. See Schmidt (1973) and Mitchell (1966).
15. Cf. McClelland (1963).
16. Moller (1978) and Moller (part 5, 1972:165).
17. See Lloyd (1966:35) and Plotnicov (1970:280).
18. See Pauw (1980:38).
19. See Lloyd (1966:37) and Plotnicov (1970:288–90).
20. See Kies (1982:16–19).
21. See Fouche (1980:34).
22. See AMPS (1985-1986).
23. See Goldthorpe (1955).
24. AMPS (1985-1986).
25. See Kies (1982:27).
26. See Kies (1982:27).
27. See AMPS (1985-1986).
28. See Plotnicov (1970:279) and Hopkins (1971:73).
29. See Manwaring (1978), Dekmejian (1971:187), Wenner (1975:175) and Frey (1965:67).
30. For example, Mkele (1961), Motshologane (1980), Marais and Van der Kooy (1980), Durand (1970), Van der Walt (1977), Koornhof (1984) and Pauw (1980).
31. For example, Lloyd (1966) in respect of Tropical Africa, Plotnicov (1970) in respect of Nigeria, Lukhero (1966) in respect of Harare, Goldthorpe (1955) in respect of Uganda, Wallerstein (1965) in respect of French-speaking West Africa, and Mercier (1956) in respect of Senegal.

5 Traditionality

1. See Eisenstadt (1973:209-10).
2. See Pretorius (1985:74–5). Cf. also Van den Berghe (1970b).
3. See Brausch (1956).
4. See Plotnicov (1970:274).
5. For example, Mercier (1956) in respect of Senegal; Wallerstein (1965) in respect of West Africa; Plotnicov (1970) in respect of Nigeria; Goldthorpe (1984:80 *et seq.*), Eisenstadt (1973) and Lloyd (1966) in respect of Tropical Africa; Bechtold (1976) in respect of Sudan; Beteille (1967) in respect of India; Akhavi (1975) in respect of Egypt; Van Dusen (1975) in respect of Syria; Zartman (1975) in respect of Algeria; and Abu-Lughod (1967) for Africa in general.
6. See Goldthorpe (1955).
7. See Mercier (1956).
8. For example, Miller (1974), Tardits (1966) and Jahoda (1966).
9. See Plotnicov (1970:282).
10. See Mercier (1956).
11. See Plotnicov (1970:289, 297).
12. Cf. Gluckman (1965) and Mercier (1956).
13. Goldthorpe (1984:181).
14. The classification still used officially is that of Van Warmelo (1935).

15. See Seligman (1978:117–21).
16. See Lloyd (1966:31).
17. See Moller (part 1, 1972:41).
18. See Carr (1965:9).
19. Swart (1981:21).
20. See Van der Burgh (1980).
21. See De Beer and Strijdom (1983).
22. See Markinor (1986).
23. See Buthelezi Commission (1982:251).
24. See Carr (1965:76).
25. See Moller (part 1, 1972:42).
26. See Swart (1981:20).
27. See Lloyd (1966:33).
28. This explication is based on Steyn and Rip (1968), Bruwer (1963), Brandel (1958), Jeffreys (1951), Moller (part 5, 1972) and Durand (1970).
29. See Lloyd (1966:30).
30. Cf. Carr (1965:25).
31. See Carr (1965:13,19).
32. See Swart (1981:24).
33. See Durand (1970:39).
34. See Carr (1965:27).
35. For a fuller discussion see Bruwer (1963:69–71) and Lungu (1982).
36. Cf. Lungu (1982).
37. See Pauw (1974).
38. See Moller (part 5, 1972:160).
39. See Lungu (1982:31–2).
40. See De Beer and Strijdom (1983:22).
41. Swart (1981:24).
42. See Hoogvelt (1981:118).
43. See Moller (part 2, 1972:19, 30).
44. See Swart (1981:24).
45. See Carr (1965:13).

6 Socio-Political Orientations

1. Buthelezi Commission (vol. 1, 1982:197).
2. Buthelezi Commission (vol. 1, 1982:212–3).
3. See Hopkins (1971:102).
4. Buthelezi Commission (vol. 1, 1982:276).
5. See Lipset (1960:267–73).

7 Conclusion

1. See Mazrui (1986:14–16, 201).

List of Works Consulted

Abdel-malek, Anonar (1968) *Egypt: Military Society*, Random House, New York.

Abueva, Jose V. (1968) 'Social Backgrounds and Recruitment of Legislators and Administrators in a Developing Country: The Philippines', in Gehan Wijeyewardene, *Leadership and Authority*, University of Malaya Press, Singapore.

Abu-Lughod, I. (1967) 'Nationalism in a New Perspective. The African Case', in Herbert J. Spiro (ed.), *Patterns of African Development*, Prentice Hall, New Jersey.

Akhavi, Shahrough (1975) 'Egypt: Neo-Patrimonial Elite', in Frank Tachau (ed.), *Political Elites and Political Development in the Middle East*, John Wiley & Sons, New York.

AMPS: See South African Research Alliance.

Ayandele, E. A. (1974) *The Educated Elite in the Nigerian Society*, Ibadan University Press.

Baltzell, E. Digby (1966) 'Who's Who in America' and ' The Social Register', in R. Bendix and S. M. Lipset (eds), *Class, Status and Power*, Free Press, New York.

Barton, Allen H. and R. Wayne Parsons (1977) 'Measuring Belief System Structure', *Public Opinion Quarterly*, 41(2), pp. 159–80.

Barton, Raymond A., Bogdan Denitch and Charles Kadushin (1973) *Opinion-Making Elites in Yugoslavia*, Praeger, New York.

Bechtold, Peter K. (1976) *Politics in the Sudan*, Praeger Publishers, New York.

Bendix, R. and S. M. Lipset (eds) (1966) *Class, Status and Power*, Free Press, New York.

Beteille, Andre (1967) 'Elite Status Groups and Caste in Modern India', in Philip Mason (ed.), *India and Ceylon: Unity and Diversity*, Oxford University Press, London.

Bottomore, T. B. (1967) 'Cohesion and Diversion in Indian Elites', in Philip Mason (ed.), *India and Ceylon: Unity and Diversity*, Oxford University Press, London.

Bottomore, T. B. (1976) *Elites and Society*, Penguin, Middlesex.

Brandel, Mia (1958) 'Urban Lobola Attitudes: A Preliminary Report', *African Studies*, 17(1), pp. 34–50.

Brandel-Syrier, Mia (1971) *Reeftown Elite*, Routledge & Kegan Paul, London.

Brandel-Syrier, Mia (1978) *Coming Through. The Search for a New Cultural Identity*, McGraw-Hill, Johannesburg.

Brausch, G. E. J. B. (1956) 'The Problem of Elites in the Belgian Congo', *International Social Science Bulletin*, 8, pp. 452–8.

Bruwer, F. P. (1963) *Die Bantoe van Suid-Afrika*, Afrikaanse Pers, Johannesburg.

Burnham, James (1972) *The Managerial Revolution*. Greenwood Press, Connecticut.

Busia, K. A. (1956) 'The Present Situation and Aspirations of Elites in the Gold Coast', *International Social Science Bulletin*, 8, pp. 422–31.

Buthelezi Commission (1982) *Report*, vols. I and II, H & H Publications, Durban.

Carr, W. J. P. (1965) *Cultural Change in Soweto. An Urban Bantu Society*, City Council of Johannesburg.

Charton, Nancy C. J. (1976) 'Black Elites in the Transkei', *Politikon*, 3, pp. 61–74.

Cilliers, S. P. (1986a) 'Urban Insiders and Rural Outsiders', *SA Indicator*, 3(3) (Summer), pp. 5–9.

Cilliers, S. P. (1986b) 'Demise of the Dompas', *SA Indicator*, 4(1) (Winter) pp. 95–8.

Coertze, R. D. (1972a) 'Die gesinslewe in Atteridgeville', in J. F. Eloff and R. D. Coertze, *Etnografiese studies in Suidelike Afrika*, J. L. van Schaik, Pretoria.

Coertze, R. D. (1972b) 'Godsdiens in Atteridgeville', in J. F. Eloff and R. D. Coertze, *Etnografiese studies in Suidelike Afrika*, J. L. van Schaik, Pretoria.

Dahl, Robert A. (1957) 'The Concept of Power', *Behavioral Science*, 2 (July) pp. 201–15.

Dahl, Robert A. (1958) 'A Critique of the Ruling Elite Model', *American Political Science Review*, 52, pp. 463–9.

Dahl, Robert A. (1961) *Who Governs? Democracy and Power in an American City*, Yale University Press.

DcDonough, Peter (1981) *Power and Ideology in Brazil*, Princeton University Press, New Jersey.

De Beer, F. E. (1979) *Meerdoelige opname onder swartes in stedelike gebiede, 1978 – besoeke aan toordokters*, Report S-N-171, HSRC, Pretoria.

De Beer, F. E. and H. G. Strijdom (1983) *Swart mans in die PWV-gebied se bande met nasionale state*, Report S-94, HSRC, Pretoria.

Dekmejian, R. Hrair (1971) *Egypt Under Nasir*, State University of New York Press, Albany.

Durand, J. J. F. (1970) *Swartman, stad en toekoms*, Tafelberg, Cape Town.

Dye, Thomas R. and John Pickering (1974) 'Governmental and Corporate Elites: Convergence and Differentiation', *Journal of Politics*, 36, pp. 900–25.

Eisenstadt, S. N. (1966) *Modernization: Protest and Change*, Prentice Hall, New Jersey.

Epstein, Cynthia Fuchs (1973) 'Positive Effects of the Multiple Negative: Explaining the Success of Black Professional Women', *American Journal of Sociology*, 78(4) (Jan.) pp. 912–35.

Field, G. Lowell and John Higley (1980) *Elitism*, Routledge & Kegan Paul, London.

Fouche, B. (1980) 'Reading and Libraries in the Socio-Cultural Life of Urban Black Community', *Mousaion*, 11(10), Unisa, Pretoria.

Frey, Frederick W. (1965) *The Turkish Political Elite*, M. I. T. Press, Boston.

Giddens, A. (1972) 'Elites', *New Society*, 22 (Nov. 16) pp. 389–92.

Giddens, A. (1973) *The Class Structure of the Advanced Societies*, Hutchinson, London.

178 *List of Works Consulted*

Giliomee, Hermann and Lawrence Schlemmer (eds) (1985) *Up Against the Fences – Poverty, Passes and Privilege in South Africa*, David Philip, Cape Town.

Gluckman, M. (1961) 'Anthropological Problems Arising From the African Industrial Revolution', in Aidan Southall (ed.), *Social Change in Modern Africa*, Oxford University Press, London.

Gluckman, Max (1965) 'Tribalism in Modern British Central Africa', in Pierre L. Van der Berghe (ed.), *Africa. Social Problems of Change and Conflict*, Chandler Publishing Co., San Francisco.

Goldthorpe, J. E. (1955) 'An African Elite', *British Journal of Sociology*, 6(1) (Mar.) pp. 31–47.

Goldthorpe, J. E. (1974) *An Introduction to Sociology*, Cambridge University Press, London.

Goldthorpe, J. E. (1984) *The Sociology of the Third World*, Cambridge University Press, Cambridge.

Guttsman, W. L. (1963) *The British Political Elite*, Basic Books, New York.

Herskovits, Melville J. (1962) *The Human Factor in Changing Africa*, Routledge & Kegan Paul, London.

Higley, John, G. Lowell Field and Knut Groholt (1976) *Elite Structure and Ideology. A Theory with Applications to Norway*, Columbia University Press, New York.

Higley, John, Desley Deacon and Don Smart (1979) *Elites in Australia*, Routledge & Kegan Paul, London.

Hoogvelt, Ankie M. (1981) *The Sociology of Developing Societies*, Macmillan, London.

Hopkins, Raymond F. (1971) *Political Roles in a New State. Tanzania's First Decade*, Yale University Press, New Haven.

Human Sciences Research Council (1985) *The South African Society: Realities and Future Prospects*, Pretoria.

Hunter, Floyd (1962) 'Review of Dahl's Who Governs?', *Administrative Science Quarterly*, 6 (Mar.) pp. 517–19.

Hunter, Floyd (1963) *Community Power Structure*, Anchor Books, New York.

Jahoda, Gustav (1966) 'Social Aspirations, Magic and Witchcraft in Ghana: A Social-Psychological Interpretation', in P. C. Lloyd (ed.), *The New Elites of Tropical Africa*, Oxford University Press, London.

Jeffreys, M. D. W. (1951) 'Lobola is Child-Price', *African Studies*, 10(4) (Dec.) pp. 145–84.

Johnson, R. W. (1974) 'The Political Elite', *New Society*, 24 (24 Jan.) pp. 188–91.

Keller, Suzanne (1979) *Beyond the Ruling Class*, Arno Press, New York.

Kies, C. W. (1982) *Problems Relating to the Use of Leisure in Soweto: A Preliminary Survey*, Report S-76, HSRC, Pretoria.

Koornhof, A. J. (1984) 'Soweto: Contemporary Urban African Values in the Context of the Essential Institutions of Race Discrimination', unpubl. D. Phil, Oxford University.

Kuzwayo, Ellen (1985) *Call Me Woman*, Ravan Press, Johannesburg.

Lenczowski, George (1975) *Political Elites in the Middle East*, American Enterprise Institute for Public Policy Research, Washington.

Lipset, Seymour Martin (1960) *Political Man. The Social Bases of Politics*, Doubleday & Co., New York.
Lipset, Seymour Martin and Aldo Solari (1967) *Elites in Latin America*, Oxford University Press, New York.
Little, Kenneth (1956) 'Two West African Elites', *International Social Science Bulletin*, 8(3), pp. 495–8.
Lloyd, P. C. (ed.) (1966) *The New Elites of Tropical Africa*, Oxford University Press, London.
Lukhero, M. B. (1966) 'The Social Characteristics of an Emergent Elite in Harare', in P. C. Lloyd (ed.), *The New Elites of Tropical Africa*, Oxford University Press, London.
Lungu, M. T. (1982) 'Xhosa Ancestor Veneration and the Communion of Saints', unpubl. M. Theol, Unisa, Pretoria.
Mannheim, Karl (1940) *Man and Society in an Age of Reconstruction*, Harcourt Brace, New York.
Mannheim, Karl (1956) *Essays on the Sociology of Culture*, Routledge & Kegan Paul, London.
Manwaring, M. G. (1978) 'Career Patterns and Attitudes of Military-Political Elites in Brazil: Similarity and Continuity, 1964–1975', *International Journal of Comparative Sociology*, 19, pp. 235–50.
Marais, G. and R. Van der Kooy (1978) *South Africa's Urban Blacks: Problems and Challenges*, Unisa School of Business Leadership, Pretoria.
Market Research Africa (1986) Omnipoll, Press release, 8 October.
Markinor (1982) *The Markinor South African Social Value Study*, Markinor, Johannesburg, March.
Markinor (1986) *National and Ethnic Ties of 800 Urban Black Women*, Press release, 16 June.
Martins, J. H. (1986) *Income and Expenditure Patterns of Urban Black Multiple Households in Johannesburg, 1985*, Unisa Bureau for Market Research, Pretoria.
Mazrui, Ali A. (1986) *The Africans – a Triple Heritage*, BBC Publications, London.
McClelland, David C. (1963) 'The Achievement Motive in Economic Growth', in Bert F. Hoselitz and Wilbert E. Moore, *Industrialization and Society*, Unesco.
Mercier, P. (1956) 'The Evolution of Senegalese Elites', *International Social Science Bulletin*, 8, pp. 441–52.
Mercier, Paul (1965) 'On the Meaning of "Tribalism" in Black Africa', in Pierre L. Van der Berghe (ed.), *Africa. Social Problems of Change and Conflict*, Chandler Publishing Co., San Francisco.
Mercier, P. (1966) 'Elites and Political Forces', in P. C. Lloyd (ed.), *The New Elites of Tropical Africa*, Oxford University Press, London.
Michels, R. (1962) *Political Parties*, Collier Books, New York.
Miller, R. A. (1974) 'Elite Formation in Africa: Class, Culture and Coherence', *Journal of Modern African Studies*, 12 (Dec.) pp. 521–42.
Mills, C. Wright (1979) *The Power Elite*, Oxford University Press, New York.
Mitchell, J. C. (1966) 'Aspects of Occupational Prestige in a Plural Society', in P. C. Lloyd, *The New Elites of Tropical Africa*, Oxford University Press, London.

180   *List of Works Consulted*

Mkele, N. (1960) 'The Emergent African Middle Class', *Optima*, Dec., pp. 217–26.

Mkele, Nimrod (1961) 'The African Middle-Class', lecture to the Institute for the Study of Man in Africa, Johannesburg, Nov.

Mokoatle, B. N. (1978) 'The Black Entrepreneur in South Africa: A Product of Social Change', in G. Marais and R. Van der Kooy, *South Africa's Urban Blacks*, Unisa School of Business Leadership, Pretoria.

Moller, H. J. (1972) *Stedelike Bantoe en die kerk*, vols. 1–5, HSRC, Pretoria.

Moller, H. J. (1978) 'The Dilemma of the Church', in G. Marais and R. Van der Kooy, *South Africa's Urban Blacks*, Unisa School of Business Leadership, Pretoria.

Mosca, G. (1939) *The Ruling Class*, McGraw-Hill, New York.

Motshologane, S. R. (1978) 'Influence of Urbanization on the Role and Status of Husband and Wife in the Tswana Family', *South African Journal of Sociology*, 17 (Apr.) pp. 83–90.

Motshologane, S. R. (1980) 'New Lifestyles in Black Society and Quality of Life', roneoed manuscript (c1980).

Pareto, Vilfredo (1963) *The Mind and Society. A Treatise on General Sociology*, vol. 3/4, Dover Publications, New York.

Pareto, Vilfredo (1968) *The Rise and Fall of the Elites*, The Bedminster Press, New Jersey.

Parry, Geraint (1969) *Political Elites*, George Allen & Unwin, London.

Parsons, T. (1958) 'The Professions and Social Structure', in Parsons, *Essays in Sociological Theory*.

Parsons, T. (1977) *The Evolution of Societies*, Prentice Hall, New Jersey.

Pauw, B. A. (1974) 'Ancestor Beliefs and Rituals Among Urban Africans', *African Studies*, 33(2), pp. 99–110.

Pauw, B. A. (1980) *The Second Generation*, Oxford University Press, Cape Town.

Peil, Margaret (1982) *Consensus and Conflict in African Societies*, Longman, England.

Plotnicov, Leonard (1970) 'The Modern African Elite of Jos, Nigeria', in Tuden and Plotnicov (eds), *Social Stratification in Africa*, Free Press, New York.

Porter, John (1965) *Vertical Mosaic. An Analysis of Social Class and Power in Canada*, University of Toronto Press, Toronto.

Prekel, Truida (1986) 'Black Women at Work: Overcoming Double Obstacles', in R. Smollan, *Black Advancement in the South African Economy*, Macmillan, Johannesburg.

Pretorius, Louwrens (1985) 'Suid-Afrikaanse kommissies van ondersoek – 'n sosiologiese ondersoek', unpubl. D. Phil, University of Stellenbosch.

Ratinoff, Luis (1967) 'The New Urban Groups', in S. M. Lipset and Aldo Solari, *Elites in Latin America*, Oxford University Press, New York.

Reissman, Leonard (1953) 'Levels of Aspiration and Social Class', *American Sociological Review*, 18(3) (June) pp. 233–42.

Republic of South Africa, President's Council (1985) *Report of the Committee for Constitutional Affairs on an Urbanization Strategy for the RSA*, PC 3/1985.

Republiek van Suid-Afrika, Presidentsraad (1983) *Verslag van die wetens-kapskomitee oor demografiese tendense in Suid-Afrika*, PR 1/1983.
Republiek van Suid-Afrika (1984) *Verslag van die Nasionale Mannekrag-kommissie oor die tydperk 1 Januarie 1983 – 31 Desember 1983*, R. P. 41/1984.
Republic of South Africa, Central Statistical Services (1980a) *Population Census 1980, Economic Characteristics*, Report 02-80-11.
Republic of South Africa, Central Statistical Services (1980b) *Population Census 1980, Social Characteristics*, Report 02-80-12.
Republic of South Africa, Central Statistical Services *Population Census 1980* (1980c), *Geographical Distribution of the Population*, Report 02-80-01.
Republic of South Africa, Central Statistical Services (1982) *South African Statistics*.
Republic of South Africa, Central Statistical Services (1986) *Bulletin of Statistics*, vol. 20, no. 3 (Sept.).
Rip, C. M. (1960) 'The Effects of Cultural Inertia and Cultural Diffusion on the Structure and Functioning of the Bantu Family System', unpubl. M. A. thesis, Unisa.
Roberts, Geoffrey K. (1972) *West German Politics*, Macmillan, London.
Rosen, Bernard C. (1956) 'The Achievement Syndrome: A Psychocultural Dimension of Social Stratification', *American Sociological Review*, 21 (Apr.) pp. 203–11.
Rosen, Bernard C. (1959) 'Race, Ethnicity and the Achievement Syndrome', *American Sociological Review*, 24 (Oct.) pp. 47–60.
Schmidt, J. J. (1973) *Beroepsprestige onder die Bantoe in 'n stedelike ge-meenskap*, report S-N-36, HSRC, Pretoria.
Schmidt, J. J. (1975) *Lewenstyle en statusdifferensiasie onder die Pedi en Changaan binne die munisipale gebied van Pretoria: 'n Verkenning*, report S-N-62, HSRC, Pretoria.
Schmidt, J. J. (1976a) *Determining Westernization/Traditionalism Among Blacks: A Methodological Contribution*, report S-N-92, HSRC, Pretoria.
Schmidt, J. J. (1976b) *Dualisme in die stratifikasiepatrone onder stedelike swartmense*, report S-N-80, HSRC, Pretoria.
Seligman, C. G. (1978) *Races of Africa*, Oxford University Press, Oxford.
Sewell, William H., Archie O. Haller and Murray A. Strauss (1957) 'Social Status and Educational and Occupational Aspiration' *American Sociological Review*, 22(1) (Feb.) pp. 67–73.
Sewell, William H. and Vimal P. Shah (1967) 'Social Class, Parental Encour-agement and Educational Aspirations', *American Journal of Sociology*, 73, pp. 559–72.
Smit, P. and P. C. Kok (1981) *Bevolkingsherverspreiding in die RSA, 1970–1980*, Report S 82, HSRC.
Smit, P. and J. J. Booysen (1981) *Swart verstedeliking. Proses, patroon en strategie*, Tafelberg, Kaapstad.
Smith, Peter H. (1979) *Labyrinths of Power. Political Recruitment in Twen-tieth Century Mexico*, Princeton University Press, Princeton University.
South African Institute of Race Relations (1985) *Race Relations Survey 1984*, Johannesburg.

South African Research Alliance, *All Media and Products Survey (AMPS)*, *May 1985 – March 1986*, Johannesburg.

Southall, Aidan (ed.) (1961) *Social Change in Modern Africa*, Oxford University Press, London.

Steyn, Anna F. and Colin M. Rip (1968) 'The Changing Urban Bantu Family', *Journal of Marriage and the Family*, Aug., pp. 499–517.

Strijdom, H. G. and C. Van der Burgh (1980) *Rolverdeling en rolverwagting in die stedelike swart gesin – 'n verkenning*, Report S-55, HSRC, Pretoria.

Suleiman, Ezra N. (1978) *Elites in French Society*, Princeton University Press, Princeton.

Swart, C. F. (1979) *Swart Behuising: Deel I, Gesinsbehuising in Soweto*, publication C 21, RAU, Johannesburg.

Swart, C. F. (1981) *Swart Behuising: Deel II, Gesinsbehuising in verskillende woonomgewings*, publication C 25, RAU, Johannesburg.

Tachau, Frank (ed.) (1975) *Political Elites and Political Development in the Middle East*, John Wiley & Sons, New York.

Tardits, C. (1956) 'The Notion of the Elite and the Urban Social Survey in Africa', *International Social Science Bulletin*, 8(3), pp. 492–5.

Tardits, Claude (1966) 'Kinship and Social Class in Porto Novo', in P. C. Lloyd *The New Elites of Tropical Africa*, Oxford University Press, London.

Tuden, Arthur and Leonard Plotnicov (eds) (1970) *Social Stratification in Africa*, Free Press, New York.

Vallier, Ivan (1967) 'Religious Elites: Differentiation and Developments in Roman Catholicism', in S. M. Lipset and A. Solari, *Elites in Latin America*, Oxford University Press, New York.

Van den Berghe, Pierre L. (ed.) (1965) *Africa. Social Problems of Change and Conflict*, Chandler Publishing Co., San Francisco.

Van den Berghe, Pierre L. (1970a) 'South Africa, a Study in Conflict', in A. Tuden and L. Plotnicov (eds), *Social Stratification in Africa*, Free Press, New York.

Van den Berghe, Pierre L. (1970b) 'Ethnicity in South Africa', in A. Tuden and L. Plotnicov (eds), *Social Stratification in Africa*, Free Press, New York.

Van der Burgh, C. (1980) *Meerdoelige opname onder swartes in blanke grootstedelike gebiede – 1978; swart mans se bande met hul swart state. Basisgegewens*, Report S-N-197, HSRC, Pretoria.

Van der Merwe, H. W. *et al.* (1974) *White South African Elites*, Juta, Cape Town.

Van der Walt, H. E. (1977) *Die beroepsmobiliteit van swart manlike gegradueerdes*, Report PERS 259, National Institute for Personnel Research, CSIR, Johannesburg.

Van Dusen, Michael H. (1975) 'Syria: Downfall of a Traditional Elite', in Frank Tachau (ed.), *Political Elites and Political Development in the Middle East*, John Wiley & Sons.

Van Pletzen, Joyce (1984) *The Wage Structure of White Male Graduates in 1984*, Report MN-108, HSRC, Pretoria.

Van Warmelo, N. J. (1935) *A Preliminary Survey of the Bantu Tribes of South Africa*, Government Printer, Pretoria.

Vorster, David (1970) 'The Ambitions of African Workers', *Management*, Nov., pp. 59–62.

Wallerstein, Emanuel (1965) 'Elites in French Speaking West Africa', *Journal of Modern African Studies*, 3(1), pp. 1–34.

Wenner, Manfred W. (1975) 'Saudi-Arabia: Survival of Traditional Elites', in Frank Tachau (ed.), *Political Elites and Political Development in the Middle East*, John Wiley & Sons, New York.

Zartman, I. William (ed.) (1980) *Elites in the Middle East*, Praeger, New York.

Zartman, I. W. (1974) 'The Study of Elite Circulation', *Comparative Politics*, 6 (Apr.) pp. 465–88.

Zonis, Marvin (1975) 'The Political Elite of Iran: A Second Stratum', in Frank Tachau (ed.), *Political Elites and Political Development in the Middle East*, John Wiley & Sons, New York.

Index